The Christian public is indebted to Dr. Reymond for producing such a lucid and incisive volume evaluating modern misguided attempts to rejoin Protestant churches with the Roman Catholic Church. He thoughtfully works his way through both the historical and contemporary issues surrounding the two most significant documents recently attempting such an ecumenical effort – 'Evangelicals and Catholics Together' (1994) and 'The Gift of Salvation' (1998). The reader will be well-informed by this decisive, but irenic, rejection of the false notions that the Roman church is the God-ordained church on earth and that the Roman church has always embraced the biblical concept of justification by faith.

Richard L. Mayhue, ThD.
Senior Vice President and Dean
The Master's Seminary, Sun Valley
California

To
my children

* * *

May they know the joy of
rearing their children
in the true Faith
—the Reformed Faith—
which was
once for all
delivered to the saints
(Jude 3)

The Reformation's Conflict With Rome

* * * * *

Why It Must Continue!

Robert L. Reymond

Mentor

ISBN 185792 626 9

Published in 2001
by Christian Focus Publications,
Geanies House, Fearn, Ross-shire,
IV20 1TW, Great Britain

Cover design by Owen Daily

Contents

Foreword

In his treatment of the doctrine of justification, Alistair McGrath, the Oxford scholar, acknowledges that Roman Catholic doctrine, not only in the sixteenth century, but today as well, differs sharply from that of historic Protestantism. However, McGrath notes that though the views have not changed between the divided parties the perception of the significance of the debate has changed dramatically.

The Spanish Inquisition is over. The routine burning at the stake for heresy is a thing of the past. In the West, especially in America, religious toleration is the order of the day. With religious toleration has come friendlier attitudes toward those who differ in doctrine. But these changes in attitude cannot possibly mark any real change in significance. The importance of the true gospel cannot be altered by changes in cultural perspective. The doctrine of *sola fide* is no less essential to the gospel today than it was in the first century. We may deem it as less important, but this reveals more about us and our generation than it does about the gospel.

Dr. Reymond clearly demonstrates in this monograph that not only does Rome continue to offer a different gospel from that of the New Testament but also that there are several serious doctrinal differences between Roman Catholic teaching and Biblical Christianity. The issues are not tangential but systemic. Rome's doctrines of the mass, purgatory, Mariology, and the papacy are but a few matters that stand as powerful barriers to any genuine reconciliation with Reformed Christians.

This book also shows that many of these issues have been defined *de fide* by Rome since the sixteenth century and that despite the change in attitude and tone, the actual doctrinal issues that divide Rome from Evangelical Christianity have actually been exacerbated since the sixteenth century.

I am confident the reader will find this work clear, fair and accurate. I highly commend its close reading.

R. C. Sproul
Orlando 2000

Foreword

The doctrine of forensic justification through faith alone in Christ alone was at the heart of the Reformation. It constituted one of the main barriers to meaningful reconciliation between the Reformers and Rome in the 16th century. But is it still worth arguing about today?

As Robert Reymond convincingly argues, the answer must be yes. Although Roman Catholic biblical scholars (like Joseph Fitzmyer) have, in the wake of the Second Vatican Council (1962-5), virtually conceded the Protestant case concerning Paul's doctrine of justification, this concession has not found its way into Rome's official creedal teaching. And there are still vociferous Roman opponents of the Pauline doctrine, especially in America, such as Robert Sungenis. Further, Eastern Orthodoxy is proving as attractive as Rome to disenchanted Evangelicals; and Orthodoxy can be just as hostile as Rome to justification by faith. Unavoidably, therefore, the controversy must continue.

This is particularly the case when leading Evangelicals seem resolved on fudging the issue in the name of cooperation with conservative Roman Catholics against all forms of liberalism. While we should rejoice in whatever common ground we find, that does not warrant obscuring a central doctrine on which Scripture speaks so clearly: a doctrine we *must* understand correctly if we are to enjoy a properly functioning faith in Jesus Christ and a healthy assurance of God's grace. The question is intensified still more deeply when we realise that behind the still unreformed official teaching of Rome lies her claim to *authority*. Rome's view of salvation rests on her belief in the papacy as the divinely guided visible head of the Church. Are Evangelicals ready to overlook or even swallow this authority claim for the sake of unity?

Robert Reymond is to be warmly commended for producing such a lucid book on the Reformation controversy with Rome, and why that controversy must continue even today.

Dr Nick Needham
Highland Theological College
Dingwall, Ross-shire

Note to My Readers

To my Roman Catholic readers who, in God's gracious providence, are reading this monograph I would, first, like to express my heartfelt appreciation to you for taking the time to read what may be very painful for you. Second, please believe me when I say that I have no rancor toward you personally; rather, it is because I care very deeply for you that I write here what I do. Third, I would respectfully and humbly request that you become like the Bereans in Acts 17:11 and "examine the Scriptures" (and your own Catholic history) for yourself to see if what I have written here is true. If I am wrong, you will have lost nothing—indeed, you may even have benefited from the intellectual stimulation—and according to your church's post-Vatican II teaching neither am I in danger of eternal perdition, who writing as a convinced Reformed Protestant am still regarded as a brother in Christ, albeit a "separated" one. But if I am right, you will suffer the loss of your soul if your trust is divided, in keeping with your church's instruction, between Christ and anyone (Mary) or anything (the church and/or your works) else. So please, read on—particularly the Scripture verses I cite—carefully, thoughtfully and attentively.

Now a word to my readers who are professing Protestants: Just because you claim to be "Protestants" is no guarantee in itself that you are genuine Christians with your sins forgiven or that you are on your way to heaven. So you too should read—carefully, thoughtfully, and attentively— everything I have written here.

In his Encyclical letter titled *Ut Unum Sint* ("that they all may be one") (Boston, MA: Pauline, 1995) released on May 25, 1995 in which he urged full unity of faith among Christ's disciples throughout the world, Pope John Paul II enumerated the following five "absolute truths" (from his perspective) as areas needing "fuller study": "1) the relationship between Sacred Scripture, as the highest authority in matters of faith, and Sacred Tradition, as indispensable to the interpretation of the Word of God; 2) the Eucharist, as the Sacrament of the Body and Blood of Christ and the sanctifying outpouring of the Holy Spirit; 3) Ordination, as a Sacrament, to the threefold ministry of the episcopate, presbyterate, and diaconate; 4) the Magisterium of the Church, entrusted to the Pope and the Bishops in communion with him, understood as a responsibility and an authority exercised in the name of Christ for teaching and safeguarding the faith; 5) the Virgin Mary, as Mother of God and Icon of the Church, the spiritual Mother who intercedes for Christ's disciples and for all humanity." (87-89)

This monograph, out of concern for biblical truth, responds to Pope John Paul II's call for "fuller study" of these "absolute truths" as well as a response to the central issue between Roman Catholicism and the Reformation, specifically, the doctrine of justification by faith alone.

The Doctrinal Conflict Between Rome and the Reformation: Why It Must Continue!

The Central Issue Between Us: Paul's Doctrine of Justification by Faith Alone

In my Sunday School class at Coral Ridge Presbyterian Church, Fort Lauderdale, Florida in September of 1999 I observed that one who knows the teachings of Roman Catholicism on justification must conclude that the Judaizers[1] in the first-century church, against whose distortion of God's law-free gospel Paul wrote his letter to the Galatians, were Rome's forerunners. Roman Catholicism, as did the Judaizers earlier, confesses Jesus of Nazareth to be the Messiah, the divine Son of God, the risen and exalted Lord, the Giver of the Spirit, in whose name is salvation. Roman Catholicism, as did the Judaizers earlier, also confesses that Christ sits today on his Father's throne in heaven and that he will return someday in great power and glory to raise the dead and to judge the world. But Roman Catholicism, as did the Judaizers earlier, also contends that a vital faith alone in the perfect obedience and finished work of Jesus Christ accomplished in the sinner's behalf is not sufficient for his justification or right standing before God. In addition to trusting in Christ's saving work the sinner must himself perform good works, which infused works of righteousness, though initiated by grace, are nonetheless *meritorious* and contribute to his final justification. The Roman Catholic counter-reformation Council of Trent

---

[1] These Judaizers are Luke's "believers belonging to the party of the Pharisees" (Acts 15:1, 5) who should have been disciplined because of their nomist teaching but instead not only were tolerated by but were even employed to run errands for the Jerusalem leadership (Gal 2:12).

(1545-1563) states in its Sixth Session, Chapter XVI, on the fruits of justification:

> ...to those *who work well unto the end* and trust in God, eternal life is to be offered, both as a grace mercifully promised to the sons of God through Christ Jesus, and as a reward promised by God himself, *to be faithfully given to their good works and merits*...nothing further is wanting to those justified [in Rome's sense of the word] to prevent them from being considered to have, *by those very works* which have been done in God, fully satisfied the divine law according to the state of this life and *to have truly merited eternal life*. (emphasis supplied).[2]

Canons 9, 11, 12, 17, 23, 24, and 32 following the sixteen chapters on justification then declare:

> 9. If anyone says that the sinner is justified by faith alone, meaning that nothing else is required to cooperate in order to obtain the grace of justification, and that it is not in any way necessary that he be prepared and disposed by the action of his own will, let him be anathema.

---

[2] The Council of Trent expressed itself on justification in its Sixth Session (January, 1547) with sixteen chapters and thirty-three canons of anathemas. Chapters one through nine stress humankind's incapacity to save itself but confirm the necessity for the cooperation of human free will, including the resolve to receive the sacrament of baptism and to begin a new life. Chapters ten through thirteen affirm that justifying grace may be increased through obedience to God's commandments and deny that predestination to salvation can be known with certainty. Chapters fourteen through sixteen declare that justifying grace is forfeited by infidelity or by other grievous sins and must be recovered through the sacrament of penance, and that salvation is given to the justified person not only as gift but also as reward since he has meritoriously fulfilled God's law by good works performed in a state of grace.

11. If anyone says that men are justified either by the sole imputation of the justice [righteousness] of Christ or by the sole remission of sins, to the exclusion of the grace and the charity which is poured forth in their hearts by the Holy Ghost, and remains in them, or also that the grace by which we are justified is only the good will of God, let him be anathema.

12. If anyone says that justifying faith is nothing else than confidence in divine mercy, which remits sins for Christ's sake, or that it is this confidence alone that justifies us, let him be anathema.

17. If anyone says that the grace of justification is shared by those only who are predestined to life..., let him be anathema.

23. If anyone says that a man once justified can sin no more, nor lose grace, and that therefore he that falls and sins was never truly justified..., let him be anathema.

24. If anyone says that the justice [righteousness] received is not preserved and also not increased before God through good works, but that those works are merely the fruits and signs of justification obtained, but not the cause of its increase, let him be anathema.

32. If anyone says that the good works of the one justified are in such manner the gifts of God that they are not also the good merits of him justified; or that the one justified by the good works that he performs by the grace of God and the merit of Jesus Christ, whose living member he is, does not truly merit an increase of grace, eternal life, and in case he dies in grace, the attainment of eternal life itself and also an increase in glory, let him be anathema.

The 1994 *Catechism of the Catholic Church*, citing the Council of Trent (Sixth Session, Chapter VII), declares: "Justification is not only the remission of sins, but also *the sanctification and renewal of the interior man*" (paragraph 1989, emphasis supplied). Clearly, Rome declares by these statements that the Christian's faith in Jesus Christ plus his life of meritorious works leads to his justification before God, a justification, by the way, that is never completed in this life.

Over against Rome's teaching stands the consentient testimony of both classic Lutheran Protestantism and classic Reformed Protestantism that affirms that biblical justification says nothing about the subjective transformation that necessarily begins to occur within the inner life of the Christian through the progressive infusion of grace that commences with the new birth (which subjective transformation Scripture and Protestantism view as progressive sanctification). Rather, biblical justification refers to God's *wholly objective, wholly forensic judgment* concerning the sinner's standing before the Law, by which forensic judgment God declares that the penitent sinner who trusts Christ is righteous in his sight because of both the imputation of his sin to Christ on which ground he is forgiven and the imputation of Christ's perfect preceptive obedience to him on which ground he is constituted righteous before God. In other words, as Paul states:

Acts 13:38-39: "...through Jesus the forgiveness of sins is proclaimed to you. Through him everyone who believes is justified from everything you could not be justified from by the law of Moses."

Romans 3:20-22: "...no one will be declared righteous in his sight by observing the law [ἔργων νόμου, *ergōn nomou*]³; rather, through the law we become conscious of sin. But now a righteousness from God, apart from law, has been made known.... This righteousness from God comes through faith in Jesus Christ⁴ to all who believe."

Romans 3:26: "[God] justifies those who have faith in Jesus."

Romans 3:28: "For we maintain that a man is justified by faith apart from observing the law."

Romans 4:2-6: "If, in fact, Abraham was justified by works, he had something to boast about—but not before God. What does the Scripture say? 'Abraham believed God, and it was credited to him as righteousness.' Now when a man works, his wages are not credited to him as a

---

³ Paul uses the phrase ἔργα νόμου, *erga nomou*, "works of law," eight times: he affirms that no one can be justified by "works of law" (Gal 2:16 [3 times]; Rom 3:20, 28), that the Spirit is not received by "works of law" (Gal 3:2, 5), and that all those whose religious efforts are characterized by "works of law" are under the law's curse (Gal 3:10). The simple ἔργα in Rom 4:2, 6; 9:12, 32; 11:6; and Eph 2:9 almost certainly has the same meaning. Paul intends by the phrase anything done in accordance with *whatever* the law commands—the moral law no less than the ritual, the ritual no less than the moral—with the intention of achieving justification or right standing before God.

⁴ It has been often urged in recent times that the expression, "faith in Jesus Christ," should be rendered "faithfulness of Jesus Christ." While it is true that Paul's πίστεως Ἰησοῦ Χριστοῦ (*pisteōs Iēsou Christou*) can be translated either way, the traditional rendering is preferrable for two reasons: first, the close connection of Romans 4, in which Paul speaks of Abraham's personal faith by which he was declared righteous, with Romans 3 supports the traditional rendering; second, whereas Paul often teaches the need for personal faith in Christ for justification, there is not a single text that speaks unambiguously of the "faithfulness of Jesus Christ" as needful for one's justification.

gift, but as an obligation. However, to the man who does not work but trusts God who justifies the wicked,[5] his faith is credited as righteousness. David says the same thing when he speaks of the blessedness of the man to whom God credits righteousness apart from works."

Romans 4:13-14: "It was not through law that Abraham and his offspring received the promise that he would be heir of the world, but through the righteousness that comes by faith. For if those who live by law are heirs, faith has no value and the promise is worthless."

Romans 9:30-32: "What then shall we say? That the Gentiles, who did not pursue righteousness, have obtained it, a righteousness that is by faith; but Israel, who pursued a law of righteousness, has not obtained it. Why not? Because they pursued it not by faith but as if it were by works."

Romans 10:4: "Christ is the end of the law so that there may be righteousness for everyone who believes."

---

[5] On the basis of Paul's statement in Romans 4:5 to the effect that God "justifies the wicked"—the same Greek phrase as is used in the LXX in Exodus 23:7 and Isaiah 5:23 of corrupt judgments on the part of human judges which God will not tolerate—James I. Packer declares that Paul's doctrine of justification is a "startling doctrine" ("Justification" in *Evangelical Dictionary of Theology* [Grand Rapids: Baker, 1984], 595). For not only does Paul declare that God does precisely what he commanded human judges not to do but also that he does it in a manner designed "to demonstrate his justice" (Rom 3:25-26). Of course, Paul relieves what otherwise would be a problem of theodicy by teaching that God justifies the wicked on just grounds, namely, that the claims of God's law upon them have been fully satisfied by Jesus Christ's doing and dying in their stead.

Romans 11:5-6: "...there is a remnant chosen by grace. And if by grace, then it is no longer by works; if it were, grace would no longer be grace."

Galatians 2:16: "...a man is not justified by observing the law but by faith in Jesus Christ. So we, too, have put our faith in Christ Jesus that we may be justified by faith in Christ and not by observing the law, because by observing the law no one will be justified."

Galatians 3:10-11: "All who rely on observing the law are under a curse, for it is written: 'Cursed is everyone who does not continue to do everything written in the Book of the Law.' Clearly no one is justified before God by the law, because 'The righteous will live by faith.'"

Ephesians 2:8-9: "For it is by grace you have been saved, through faith—and this not from yourselves, it is the gift of God—not by works, so that no one can boast."

Philippians 3:9: "...not having a righteousness of my own that comes from the law but that [righteousness] which is through faith in Christ—the righteousness that comes from God and is by faith."

Titus 3:5, 7: "[God] saved us, not because of righteous things we had done, but because of his mercy...so that, having been justified by his grace [and if by his grace, then it is no longer by ours works—RLR], we might become heirs having the hope of eternal life."

From these verses it is plain that Paul teaches that justification is by "faith alone" (*sola fide*) in Christ's preceptive and penal obedience. The moment the penitent sinner casts himself upon God's mercies in Christ, God *pardons* him of all his sins (Acts 10:43; Rom 4:6-7)[6] and *constitutes* him righteous before him by imputing or reckoning the righteousness of Christ to him (Rom 5:1, 19; 2 Cor 5:21).[7] And on the basis of his *constituting* the ungodly man righteous by his act of imputation, God simultaneously *declares* the ungodly man to be righteous in his sight. The now-justified ungodly man is then, to employ Luther's expression, *simul iustus et peccator* ("simultaneously a righteous man and a sinner"). The doctrine of justification means then that in God's sight the ungodly man, now "in Christ," has perfectly kept the moral law of God, which also means that "in Christ" the penitent sinner in God's sight has perfectly loved God with all his heart, soul, mind, and strength and his neighbor as himself.

Quite correctly then did Martin Luther declare that the Pauline doctrine of justification by faith alone, that is, by faith in Christ apart from all our works, is the article of the standing or falling church (*articulus stantis vel cadentis ecclesiae*).[8] John Calvin declared it to be "the main hinge on

---

[6] See Acts 10:43—"...everyone who believes *has received* [λαβεῖν, *labein*] forgiveness of sins," and Romans 4:6-7—"David says the same thing when he speaks of the blessedness of the man to whom God *credits righteousness apart from works:* 'Blessed are they whose transgressions are forgiven [ἀφέθησαν, *aphethēsan*], whose sins *are covered* [ἐπεκαλύφθησαν, *epekaluphthēsan*].'"

[7] See Romans 5:1—"...*having been justified* [δικαιωθέντες, *dikaiōthentes*] by faith," 5:19—"...so also through the obedience of the one man the many *shall be constituted* [κατασταθήσονται, *katastathēsontai*] righteous," and 2 Cor 5:21—"God made him who had no sin to be sin for us, so that in him we might become the righteousness of God."

[8] See Luther's exposition of Psalm 130:4 in his *Werke* (Weimar: Böhlau, 1883 to present), 40/3:352, 3: "...*quia isto articulo stante stat Ecclesia, ruente ruit Ecclesia.*"

which religion turns",[9] "the sum of all piety,"[10] and the "first and keenest subject of controversy"[11] between Rome and the Reformation.

I noted too for my Sunday School class that Rome's unevangelical, anti-Pauline nomism—one may justly label its nomism a form of "legalism"—it has never repudiated. Indeed, Rome continues to this day to urge upon the world the teachings of Trent,[12] thus evidencing its own apostate condition. Paul condemned the Judaizers' teaching in his day,[13] and were he living today he would denounce in equally

---

[9] John Calvin, *Institutes of the Christian Religion*, 3.11.1.

[10] Calvin, *Institutes*, 3.15.7.

[11] John Calvin, "Reply to Sadoleto," *A Reformation Debate* (Grand Rapids: Baker, 1966), 66. Not only does Calvin declare the doctrine of justification by faith apart from works to be the "first and keenest subject of controversy" between Rome and the Reformation but he also asserts in the same context that "wherever the knowledge of it is taken away, the glory of Christ is extinguished, religion abolished, the Church destroyed, and the hope of salvation utterly overthrown."

[12] Lest one conclude that Rome does not take Trent's deliverances seriously anymore, he should consider the following citation from the 1994 publication, the *Catechism of the Catholic Church*: citing the Council of Trent (Sixth Session, Chapter VII, 1547), it declares: "Justification is not only the remission of sins, but also *the sanctification and renewal of the interior man*" (para. 1989, emphasis supplied). It also states: "Justification is conferred in Baptism" and by it God "*makes us inwardly just* by the power of his mercy" (para. 1992, emphasis supplied). This catechetical deliverance and the following statement of Pope John Paul II, made in his 1995 address commemorating the 450th anniversary of the Council of Trent, should be sufficient to demonstrate that Rome does indeed still espouse Trent's teaching on justification:

> Thus, with the Decree of Justification—one of the most valuable achievements for the formulation of Catholic doctrine—the council intended to safeguard the role assigned by Christ to the Church and her sacraments in the process of sinful man's justification.

[13] Paul twice calls down God's "anathema" on the Judaizers who

condemnatory terms the teachings of Rome as well. One of the members of my class asked me: "Since its teachings are so obviously non-Pauline, why does Rome teach what it does about justification?" My answer that

were "trying to pervert the gospel of Christ" by their law-ridden "gospel, which is really no gospel at all" (Gal 1:8-9). His words deserve citation:

...even if we or an angel from heaven should preach a gospel other than the one we preached to you, let him be eternally condemned [ἀνάθεμα ἔστω, *anathema estō*]! As we have already said, so now I say again: If anybody is preaching to you a gospel other than what you accepted, let him be eternally condemned [ἀνάθεμα ἔστω, *anathema estō*]!

The first thing that must be noted from Paul's statement is that for him the gospel—justification by faith alone in Christ's saving work—was already a *fixed* message needing no additions or alterations to it in the mid-first century when he first came to the Galatian region and proclaimed it. Neither he nor an angel from heaven could alter it in any way or to any degree without falling under divine condemnation. The implication of Paul's statement here is clear: irrespective of *whatever else* they may believe—including even *every* tenet of the Apostles' Creed—they who would teach others that in order to be justified before God and thus go to heaven when they die they must, in addition to trusting Christ's saving work, "keep the law," that is, perform meritorious good works of their own, are in actuality "false brothers" and stand under God's condemnation. Rome's Tradition, which has corrupted the law-free gospel with its many additions, falls under such condemnation. In fact, the sad truth is that from the post-apostolic age to the present time many church fathers and many church communions, in addition to the Roman Catholic Church, have proclaimed "a different gospel" and thus stand under Paul's apostolic anathema.

As for the word "anathema" (ἀνάθεμα, *anathema*), it is derived from the preposition ἀνά (*ana*, "up"), the verb τίθημι (*tithēmi*, "to place or set"), and the -μα (*-ma*) noun ending conveying passive voice significance. Hence it refers to "something set or placed up [before God]" and is the New Testament synonym of the Old Testament חרם (*cherem*, "devoted") principle of "devoting" or handing something or someone over to God for his disposal, usually to destruction.

morning was somewhat sparse due to time: *"Rome has followed its Tradition and that Tradition has been for the most part bad Tradition."* But thinking that many Protestants (and, I sincerely hope, many Roman Catholics as well) might have the same question, I have expanded upon my answer here.[14]

Rome's Twofold Authority

From the vantage point of the great sixteenth-century magisterial Reformation, one must conclude that the Roman Catholic Church's problems in the area of soteriology (and there are many) begin in the arena of authority. Protestantism has one authority—the inspired Scriptures of the Old and New Testaments. Rome has two authorities—Scripture and Tradition—and Protestantism disagrees with Rome's understanding of, teaching on, and interpretation of both.

Rome's View of Scripture

With respect to its view of Scripture, Rome places twelve additional Apocryphal ("hidden," then "obscure," then "spurious") books within the Old Testament, namely, Tobit, Judith, the (six) Additions to the Book of Esther, the Wisdom of Solomon, the Wisdom of Jesus the Son of Sirach (known also as Ecclesiasticus), Baruch, the Letter of Jeremiah, the Prayer of Azariah and the Song of the Three Young Men (considered one work), Susanna, Bel and the

---

[14] I would urge the reader who is interested in seriously researching Roman Catholicism beyond these pages to begin with Loraine Boettner's *Roman Catholicism* (Philadelphia: Presbyterian and Reformed, 1970), then to turn to Gerrit C. Berkouwer's somewhat dated *The Conflict with Rome* (Philadelphia: Presbyterian and Reformed, 1958) and then to John W. Robbins' *Ecclesiastical Megalomania* (Unicoi, Tenn.: Trinity Foundation, 1999).

Dragon, and 1 and 2 Maccabees. Bruce M. Metzger, professor emeritus of New Testament at Princeton Seminary, in his editorial "Introduction to the Apocrypha" in *The Oxford Annotated Apocrypha*, explains how these books came to be included by Rome in its Old Testament canon:

At the end of the fourth century Pope Damasus commissioned Jerome, the most learned biblical scholar of his day, to prepare a standard Latin version of the Scriptures (the Latin Vulgate). In the Old Testament Jerome followed the Hebrew canon and by means of prefaces called the reader's attention to the separate category of the apocryphal books [In the preface to his Latin Version of the Bible Jerome, after translating the thirty-nine books of the Old Testament, says: "Anything outside of these must be placed within the Apocrypha," that is, within the non-canonical books.]. Subsequent copyists of the Latin Bible, however, were not always careful to transmit Jerome's prefaces, and during the medieval period the Western Church generally regarded these books as part of the holy Scriptures. [At one of its prolonged sessions which occurred on April 8, 1546, with only fifty-three prelates present, not one of whom was a scholar distinguished for historical learning—RLR]...the Council of Trent decreed [in its "Sacrosancta"] that the canon of the Old Testament includes them (except the Prayer of Manasseh and 1 and 2 Esdras) [and, I may add, Trent went on to anathematize any one who "does not accept these entire books, with all their parts, as they have customarily been read in the Catholic Church and are found in the ancient editions of the Latin Vulgate, as sacred and canonical." This decree was confirmed by Vatican I (1870). RLR]. Subsequent editions of the Latin Vulgate text, officially approved by the Roman Catholic

Church, contain these books incorporated within the sequence of the Old Testament books. Thus Tobit and Judith stand after Nehemiah; the Wisdom of Solomon and Ecclesiasticus stand after the Song of Solomon; Baruch (with the Letter of Jeremiah as chapter 6) stands after Lamentations; and 1 and 2 Maccabees conclude the books of the Old Testament. [Metzger could have also noted that the Prayer of Azariah and the Song of the Three Young Men is placed between Daniel 3:23 and 3:24; Susanna is placed either at the beginning of Daniel as an introduction to chapter 1 (this placement is that of the Greek text of Theodotian and the Old Latin, Coptic, and Arabic versions) or at the end of Daniel as chapter 13 (this placement is that of the Septuagint and the Latin Vulgate); and Bel and the Dragon is placed either at the close of Daniel 12 in the Greek manuscripts of Daniel or at the end of Daniel as chapter 14 in the Latin Vulgate, Susanna being chapter 13.—RLR] An appendix after the New Testament contains the Prayer of Manasseh and 1 and 2 Esdras, without implying canonical status.

...Thus Roman Catholics accept as fully canonical those books and parts of books which Protestants call the Apocrypha (except the Prayer of Manasseh and 1 and 2 Esdras, which both groups regard as apocryphal). [15]

What should we say about these additions to the Old Testament canon? To begin, these Apocryphal books were written predominantly in Greek (Tobit, Judith, Ecclesiasticus, part of Baruch, and 1 Maccabees are the exceptions here, having been written in Hebrew or, in part at least, in Aramaic), during the last two centuries before Christ and the first century of the Christian era *long after the Hebrew*

---

[15] Bruce M. Metzger, "Introduction to the Apocrypha" in *The Oxford Annotated Apocrypha* (New York: Oxford University, 1965), x-xi.

Old Testament canon was completed. Interestingly, these books themselves, from first to last, bear testimony to the assertion of the Jewish historian Josephus (*Against Apion,* 1.8) that "an exact succession of the prophets" had been broken after the close of the Hebrew canon of the Old Testament. Not only is the phrase, "Thus says the Lord," which occurs so frequently in the Old Testament, nowhere to be found in them but also divine authority is never claimed by their authors for these books and by some of them it is virtually disowned, as is suggested by the following citations:

1 Maccabees 9:27: "...there was great distress in Israel [in the time of the author], such as had not been since the time that prophets had ceased to appear among them."

1 Maccabees 14:41: "...the Jews and their priests decided that Simon [Maccabeus] should be their leader and high priest in perpetuity, until a trustworthy prophet should arise." (See also here 1 Maccabees 4:46: "...until there should come a prophet...")

2 Maccabees 2:23; 15:37-38: "...all this, which has been set forth by Jason of Cyrene in five volumes, we shall attempt to condense into a single book [that is, 2 Maccabees itself]...So I too will here end my story. If it is well told and to the point, that is what I myself desired; if it is poorly done and mediocre, that was the best I could do."

Moreover, Malachi, the last canonical Old Testament prophet, predicted that the next messenger God would send to Israel as the forerunner of the Messiah would be Elijah the prophet (Mal 3:1; 4:5), which prophecy the New Testament teaches was fulfilled by the birth and ministry of John the Baptist (Mark 1:2; Matt 11:10-14; 17:11-13).

Accordingly, the Palestinian Jews never accepted these Apocryphal books as canonical, their canon being essentially the same as that of the Protestant Old Testament today (see Josephus, *Against Apion*, 1.41; *Babylonian Talmud*, Yomah 9b, Sota 48b, Sanhedrin 11a). Nor did Jesus or the New Testament writers ever cite from these books. When Paul declared then that the Jews possessed "the oracles of God" (Rom 3:2), he was implicitly excluding the Apocrypha from those "oracles."

According to Gleason L. Archer, Jr., professor emeritus of Old Testament and Semitic languages at Trinity Evangelical Divinity School, the Septuagint—the pre-Christian Alexandrian Jewish translation of the Hebrew Old Testament—was the only ancient version which included in one manuscript tradition or another the books of the Apocrypha. This has led some scholars to speak of an "Alexandrian Canon" which held equal authority among Jews along with the "Palestinian Canon." But, writes Archer, while Philo of Alexandria "quotes frequently from the canonical books of the 'Palestinian Canon,' he never once quotes from any of the apocryphal books." Furthermore, Aquila's Greek version, even though it did not contain the Apocrypha, was accepted by Alexandrian Jews in the second century A.D. Jerome explained the presence of the Apocrypha in the Alexandrian version by saying that the Alexandrian Jews included in their edition of the Old Testament both the canonical books and the books which were "ecclesiastical" (that is, considered valuable though not inspired).[16] And as I just said, while it is true that the Septuagint served as the Greek "Bible" of the early church and of the apostles in their mission to the Gentiles, there is no evidence that a New Testament writer cites from any of the Apocryphal books. It

---

[16] Gleason L. Archer, Jr., *A Survey of Old Testament Introduction* (Revised edition; Chicago: Moody, 1994), 81-2.

must also be noted that these books abound in historical, geographical, and chronological inaccuracies and anachronisms which would not occur in divinely inspired documents. Consider the following historical inaccuracies:

1. In 1 Maccabees 8:1-16 the author describes the power of Rome. His description contains many inaccuracies such as (1) his statement in verse 8 that Antiochus the Great surrendered Media and India to the Romans when in fact he kept Media and India was not even part of Antiochus' domain; (2) his statement in verse 12 that the Romans "kept friendship" with those who rely on them which simply was not true; (3) his statement in verse 15 that three hundred and twenty (actually three hundred, but this could be the author's "rounding" of a number which should not be faulted) Roman senators deliberate daily in matters of government when in fact they met three times a month and on festival days; and (4) his statement in verse 16 that the Roman senate trusted one man each year to rule over them with no envy or jealousy existing among them when "in fact, to prevent the concentration of power in one man's hands they elected two collegiate chief magistrates (consuls) year by year, each of whom had the right of veto over the others proceedings,"[17] and envy and jealousy among them were constant.

2. Tobit 1:4-5 teaches that the division of the kingdom (under Jeroboam I in 931 B.C.) occurred when Tobit was a "young man." But Tobit is also said to be a young Israelite captive living in Nineveh under Shalmaneser in the late eighth century B.C. This would make him as a "young man" almost two hundred years old at the time of the Assyrian Captivity and he lived into the reign of Esarhaddon (680-668 B.C.).

---

[17] F. F. Bruce, *Paul: Apostle of the Heart Set Free* (Reprint; Grand Rapids: Eerdmans, 1996), 24.

But according to Tobit 14:11 he died when he was one hundred and fifty-eight years old (according to the Latin text, he died at one hundred and two).

3. Judith 1:1 declares that Nebuchadnezzar reigned over the Assyrians at Nineveh at the time that Arphaxad reigned over the Medes in Ecbatana. But Nebuchadnezzar did not reign over the Assyrians at Nineveh; he was the second king of the Neo-Babylonian Empire reigning at Babylon. Arphaxad is unknown.

These books also teach doctrines which are at variance with the inspired Scriptures. For example, 2 Maccabees 12:43-45 teaches the efficacy of prayers and offerings for the dead.[18] Ecclesiasticus 3:30 teaches that almsgiving makes atonement for sin and justifies cruelty to slaves (33:26, 28). The Wisdom of Solomon teaches the doctrine of emanation (7:25) and the Platonic doctrine of the pre-existence of souls (8:18-20).

Accordingly, the Dutch Bible published by Jacob van Liesveldt at Antwerp (1526) placed the Apocryphal books after Malachi and identified the section as "the books which are not in the canon, that is to say, which one does not find among the Jews in the Hebrew." The six-volume Swiss-

---

[18] The Roman Catholic Church bases its doctrine of purgatory and Masses for the dead primarily upon this apocryphal passage, but a close examination of this passage shows that it does not support Rome's teaching. Rome teaches that at death only those Christians go to purgatory who have only venial and no unforgiven mortal sin against their souls. But the dead soldiers in the Maccabees context fell in battle because "under the tunic of every one of the dead [were] found sacred tokens of the idols of Jamnia" (12:40), that is to say, they were idolaters and thus guilty of violating the first commandment—a mortal sin! They would therefore have already been consigned to hell, and would not have been in purgatory.

German Bible (1527-29) placed the Apocryphal books in the fifth volume, the title page of which volume reads: "These are the books which are not reckoned as biblical by the ancients, nor are found among the Hebrews." Concerned to return to the sole authority of inspired, inerrant Scripture, Martin Luther in his German translation of the Bible (1534) placed the Apocryphal books once again between the Old and New Testaments with the title: "Apocrypha, that is, books which are not held equal to the sacred Scriptures, and nevertheless are useful and good to read." Miles Coverdale's English translation of the Bible (1535) put them in the same position with the title: "Apocrypha. The books and treatises which among the fathers of old are not reckoned to be of like authority with the other books of the Bible, neither are they found in the Canon of the Old Testament." *The Thirty-Nine Articles* of the Church of England (1562) state concerning the Apocrypha: "And the other books (as Jerome saith) the Church doth read for example of life, and instruction of manners; but yet doth it not apply them to establish any doctrine." And the *Westminster Confession of Faith* (1648) declares: "The books commonly called Apocrypha, not being of divine inspiration, are no part of the canon of Scripture; and therefore are of no authority in the Church of God, nor to be otherwise approved, or made use of, than other human writings" (I.3).[19]

Then because of its views on Tradition Rome also rejects most of the great attributes of canonical Scripture which

---

[19] Merrill F. Unger, *Introductory Guide to the Old Testament* (Grand Rapids: Zondervan, 1956), 81-114, treats the phenomena of the Apocrypha which make it evident that these books are not products of the Holy Spirit's inspiration. See also R. Laird Harris, *Inspiration and Canonicity of the Bible* (Grand Rapids: Zondervan, 1957), Chapters 6, 8, and Roger Beckwith, *The Old Testament Canon of the New Testament Church and Its Background in Early Judaism* (Grand Rapids: Eerdmans, 1986), 338-437.

Protestantism holds in the highest esteem, namely, Scripture's self-canonization,[20] its inerrancy, its necessity, its self-attestation, its sufficiency, its perspicuity, and its finality. So historic Protestantism and Roman Catholicism do not share the same Bible, either *extensively* as to the number of books or *intensively* as to the nature of Holy Scripture itself. For Protestantism the Bible alone (*sola scriptura*) is self-validating and absolutely authoritative in all matters of faith and practice; for Roman Catholicism its enlarged Bible (and this applies to any given statement in it) has only the meaning and thus the authority the Roman Church has determined to grant to it at any given moment.

Rome's View of Tradition

With respect to its view of Tradition, which Protestantism rejects as having no authority in the church equal to that of Holy Scripture, Rome insists that its Tradition possesses an authority equal to that of Scripture itself and that the church should receive and venerate its Tradition with the same feeling of piety and reverence that it feels for the Old and New Testaments.[21] Very cleverly, the *Catechism of the*

---

[20] Rome declares that it is the church that gave to the world the Scriptures, whereas Protestants contend that the Scriptures gave to the world the church. For my full treatment of this matter, see "The Formation and Close of the Church's Canon," in my *A New Systematic Theology of the Christian Faith* (Nashville, Tenn: Thomas Nelson, 1998), 60-70.

[21] Vatican II's *Dei Verbum*, 9 (November 1965), declares that the church "does not derive her certainty about all revealed truths from the holy Scriptures alone. Both Scripture and Tradition must be *accepted and honored with equal sentiments of devotion and reverence*" (emphasis supplied). It is theological reaching of the worst kind when some over-zealous Roman Catholic apologists find in the statements of John 20:30 and 21:25 grounds for that communion's many later traditions which contradict New Testament teaching.

Catholic Church (1994) blurs the distinction between canonical revelation (which is indisputably authoritative) and Rome's own later traditions (which are non-canonical and therefore not authoritative) when it declares:

> The Tradition here in question comes from the apostles and hands on what they received from Jesus' teaching and example and what they learned from the Holy Spirit. The first generation of Christians did not yet have a written New Testament, and the New Testament itself demonstrates the process of living Tradition. (Para. 83)

It is true, of course, that the first Christians did not have a written New Testament, but they did have the Old Testament and inspired apostles living among them to give them authoritative *revelational* instruction which is referred to as "the traditions" (τὰς παραδόσεις, *tas paradoseis*, lit., "the things passed on") in 2 Thessalonians 2:15. But it is a giant leap in logic and theological "reaching" of the worst kind simply to assert, because there was such a thing as "*apostolic* tradition" coming *directly* from the apostles in the New Testament age, that the fact of *that* inspired "tradition" justifies Rome's claim to an ongoing, perpetual "process of living Tradition" within its communion throughout the present age whose authority is on a par with Scripture's authority.

The problem with this dual authority of Scripture and Tradition, of course, is that the Scriptures cannot (and in fact do not) really govern the content of Tradition, not to mention the fact that with this view of Tradition, given Rome's view of itself as a *living* organism in its capacity as the "depository of Tradition," there can never be a codification of or limitation placed upon the content of this Tradition, not even by Scripture. As Charles Elliot states: "...so far as we are aware, there is no publication which contains a summary of what the Church believes under the head of tradition."[22] As a result, because Rome's Tradition is ever free to include doctrines which are the very antithesis of Scripture teaching while yet claiming divine authority—becoming thereby bad tradition as recent history will verify (consider the papal dogmas of the Immaculate Conception in 1854, papal infallibility in 1870, and the Assumption of Mary in 1950)—the church is left vulnerable to every kind of innovation. Moreover, Rome's teaching on Tradition impiously implies, since Protestantism self-consciously rejects one of the two "indispensable media of divine revelation," that Protestantism cannot possibly be the church of Christ, when in fact it is Rome with its dogmatic deliverances from the Council of Trent to the present day that is perverting Christian truth by its "traditions of men."

The Papacy and Papal Infallibility

In this connection I must say something about Rome's doctrine of the papacy and papal infallibility, declared to be church dogma in 1870 at the First Vatican Council, which is a major aspect of its more recent Tradition and which contributes in a very significant way, for Roman Catholic belief, to the authority of its Tradition.[23]

The Roman Catholic Church since the early Middle Ages has contended that in Matthew 16:18 Jesus declared that Peter was to be the first pope (of Rome, of course) and as such the supreme leader of Christendom, and that his

---

[22] Charles Elliot, *Delineation of Roman Catholicism* (London: J. Mason, 1851), 40.

[23] Because Rome understands the church to consist in the Roman *curia* or papal court and cardinals, bishops, and priests but not the laity, it must be understood that when Pope John Paul II issues apologies for that church's historical failings such as its forced conversions and anti-Semitism in the past, he does not mean that the "infallible church"—

supremacy would be transmitted in seamless succession to each bishop of Rome who would succeed him. This contention is dramatically captured by the Latin inscription around the entablature just below the great dome of Saint Peter's Basilica in Rome: *Tu es Petrus, et super hanc petram aedificabo Ecclesiam meam.*[24] Accordingly, the Roman Catholic *Baltimore Catechism* states:

> Christ gave special powers in His Church to St. Peter by making him the head of the Apostles and the chief teacher and ruler of the entire Church. Christ did not intend that the special power of chief teacher and ruler of the entire Church should be exercised by St. Peter alone, but intended that this power should be passed down to his successor, the Pope, the Bishop of Rome, who is the Vicar of Christ on earth and the visible head of the Church.[25]

---

that is, the papacy and the Roman *curia*—is guilty, for it is always "holy and immaculate." Rather he intends that such sins of the past were committed by the church's "sons and daughters." Here is a classic example of Rome's casuistry.

[24] Rome also claims that St. Peter's Basilica is built over Peter's grave site. In his Christmas message delivered on December 23, 1950, Pope Pius XII announced, as a result of excavations carried out in 1939 under St. Peter's Basilica, that "the grave of the Prince of Apostles has been found." Oscar Cullmann, in his *Peter: Disciple—Apostle—Martyr* (Philadelphia: Westminster, 1953), after carefully examining the written reports of this excavation, concluded:

> The archaeological investigations do not permit us to answer in either a negative or an affirmative way the question as to the stay of Peter in Rome. The grave of Peter cannot be identified. The real proofs for the martyrdom of Peter in Rome must still be derived from the indirect literary witnesses.... (153)

[25] *Baltimore Catechism. The New Confraternity Edition of the Official Revised 1949 Edition* (New York: Benzinger, 1952). The *Catechism of the Catholic Church* (1994) also states in this same regard:

And the Roman Catholic Church has employed this dogma to claim for itself the authority to bind men's consciences by its interpretation of Scripture, to add new doctrines not taught in the Scripture, and to reinterpret the plain teaching of Scripture. It has done so, as we have suggested, by first distinguishing Peter from the other apostles and then by claiming that his apostolic authority is continued in the single unbroken line of the Bishops of Rome.

Now it is true that in the early years of the New Testament era Peter was a leader among the apostles. A case can even be made that he was the "first among equals" (*primus inter pares*) in some sense.[26] Consider the following data. There

---

The Lord made Simon alone, whom he named Peter, the "rock" of his Church. He gave him the keys of his Church and instituted him shepherd of the whole flock. "The office of binding and loosing which was given to Peter was also assigned to the college of apostles united to its head." This pastoral office of Peter and the other apostles belongs to the Church's very foundation and is continued by the bishops under the primacy of the Pope.

The *Pope*, Bishop of Rome and Peter's successor, "is the perpetual and visible source and foundation of the unity both of the bishops and of the whole company of the faithful." "...the Roman Pontiff, by reason of his office as Vicar of Christ, and as pastor of the entire Church has full, supreme, and universal power over the whole Church, a power which he can always exercise unhindered." (para. 881-2)

The Protestant position on this matter is stated clearly in *Westminster Confession of Faith*, XXV/vi:

There is no other head of the Church but the Lord Jesus Christ: nor can the Pope of Rome in any sense be the head thereof; but is that Antichrist, that man of sin and son of perdition, that exalteth himself in the Church against Christ, and all that is called God.

[26] While happily conceding this, we deny that Peter ever held among the apostles any "primacy of power" (*primatus potestatis*).

are around one hundred and forty references to Peter in the four Gospels, some thirty more times than all the references to the other disciples combined. He stands at the head of the list of the twelve apostles in each of the lists given in the New Testament (Matt 10:2 [note Matthew's "first" here]; Mark 3:16; Luke 6:14; Acts 1:13), and he is included among that "inner circle" of disciples (Peter, James, and John) which alone witnessed certain miraculous events such as Jesus' transfiguration; he is the spokesman for the disciples on many occasions (Matt 15:15; 17:24-25; 19:27; John 6:68-69); it is he who walked with Jesus on the sea (Matt 14:28-29); it is he whom Jesus specifically charged to "strengthen your brothers" (Luke 22:32). He was in charge in the selection of the one to take Judas's place in Acts 1; it was he who preached the first "Christian sermon" on the Day of Pentecost in Acts 2, converting many Jews to the Way; it was his activities (along with John's) which Luke recounts in the first half of Acts; it was he whom God chose to be the missionary who would take the special action with regard to Cornelius' household in behalf of Gentile salvation in Acts 10; his was the first testimony to be recounted by Luke at the assembly in Jerusalem in Acts 15; his name appears first in Paul's "official list"[27] of those to whom Christ appeared after his resurrection (1 Cor 15:5); and Paul even refers to him (along with James and John) as a "pillar" (στύλος, *stulos*) in the church at Jerusalem (Gal 2:9). All this is beyond dispute. But to derive Rome's understanding of Peter's priority, which goes beyond what the New Testament actually teaches about it, from Matthew 16:18 (Rome bolsters its position with a few related verses such

---

[27] An unabridged list would have included Jesus' appearances first to the women as they hurried away from the tomb (Matt 28:8-9) and then to Mary who followed Peter and John back to the tomb after informing them that the tomb was empty (see John 20:1-18).

as Luke 22:31-32 and John 21:16) forces the verse to say something which it does not say. For the verse to bear such heavy doctrinal weight, the Roman Catholic apologist must demonstrate the following things *exegetically* and not simply assert them dogmatically:

1. That by his reference to "this rock" in his explanation Jesus referred to Peter personally and exclusively in his office as an apostle to the total exclusion of the other apostles;

2. That the unique authority which belongs to the apostolic office in the New Testament and in this case to Peter in particular *could* be transmitted, that is, was *transmissible*, to his "papal successors" and was *in fact* transmitted to his successors; and that the unique apostolic authority which the other apostles also possessed could *not* be and in fact was *not* transmitted, that is to say, was *non-transmissible*, to their successors;

3. That Jesus intended his promise to Peter *in fact* to extend in a repetitive way to Peter's "papal successors" throughout the entire period of the church to the end of the age; and

4. That Jesus' promise to Peter, while it could and should be *chronologically* extended to his "papal successors," cannot be *geographically* extended but must rather be restricted in its transmissibility only to one (at a time) bishop who ministers in *one* particular city among the many cities in which Peter doubtless ministered, namely, to the bishop of Rome. John Calvin made this point this way: "By what right do [the Roman apologists] bind to a [specific] place this dignity which has been given without mention of place?" (*Institutes*, IV.vi.11).

The Roman Catholic apologist must also be able to

demonstrate *historically* that Peter in fact became the first bishop of Rome and not simply assert it dogmatically. But what are the facts? Irenaeus and Eusebius of Caesarea both make Linus, mentioned in 2 Timothy 4:21, the first bishop of Rome.[28] That Peter may have died, as ancient tradition has it, in Rome is a distinct possibility (see 1 Peter 5:13 where "Babylon" has been rather uniformly understood by modern commentators as a metaphor for Rome), but that he ever actually pastored the church there is a blatant fiction which the more candid scholars in the Roman communion will acknowledge. Jerome's Latin translation of Eusebius (not Eusebius' Greek copy) records that Peter ministered in Rome for twenty-five years, but if Philip Schaff (as well as many other church historians) is to be believed, this is "a colossal chronological mistake."[29] Consider: Paul wrote his letter to the church in Rome in early A.D. 57, but he did not address the letter to Peter or refer to him anywhere in it as its pastor. And in the last chapter he extended greetings to no less than twenty-six specific friends in the Imperial city but he makes no mention of Peter which would have been a major oversight, indeed an affront to Peter, if in fact Peter were "ruling" the Roman church at that time. Then later when Paul was himself in Rome, from which city he wrote both his four prison letters during his first imprisonment in A.D. 60-62 when he "was welcoming all who came to him" (Acts 28:30), and his last pastoral letter during his second imprisonment around A.D. 64, in which letters he extended greetings to his letters' recipients from ten specific people in Rome, again he makes no mention of Peter being there. Here is a period of time spanning around seven years (A.D.

---

[28] Irenaeus does so in his *Against Heresies*, III.iii.3; Eusebius, probably following Irenaeus' lead, does so in his *Ecclesiastical History*, III.ii.

[29] Philip Schaff, *History of the Christian Church* (Grand Rapids: Eerdmans, 1962 reprint of the 1910 edition), I, 252.

57-64) during which time Paul related himself to the Roman church both as correspondent and as resident, but he says not a word which would suggest that he believed Peter was in Rome. What are we to make of Paul's silence? And if Peter was at Rome and was simply not mentioned by Paul in any of these letters, what are we to conclude about him when Paul declares to the Philippians: "I have no one else [besides Timothy] of kindred spirit who will genuinely be concerned for your welfare. For they all seek after their own interests, not those of Christ Jesus" (Phil 2:20-21), or when he writes to Timothy later and says: "Only Luke is with me.... At my first defense no one supported me, but all deserted me" (2 Tim 4:11, 16)? And what are we to make of an alleged extended ministry on Peter's part *in Rome* in light of Paul's statement in Galatians 2:7-8 that the apostolate had entrusted Peter with missionary efforts to Jews? Are we to conclude that Peter had been disobedient to that trust? I think not. For just as Paul wrote several of his letters to churches he had founded, so it would appear that Peter also, writing from Babylon to dispersed Jewish Christians (see his use of διασπορά [*diaspora*] in 1 Peter 1:1) in Pontus, Galatia, Cappadocia, Asia and Bithynia, was writing to people he had evangelized in those places. The one glimpse we have from Paul's writings concerning Peter's whereabouts and ministry is found in 1 Corinthians 9:5 where he suggests that Cephas, his wife with him (see Matt 8:14), was an itinerant evangelist carrying out the trust which the other apostles had given him. From this data we must conclude, if Peter did in fact reach Rome as tradition says, that his purpose more than likely would have been only to pay the church there not much more than a casual visit, and that he would have arrived there only shortly before his death which, according to tradition, occurred during the Neronic persecution.

The Roman Catholic apologist must also be able to

address, to the satisfaction of reasonable men, the following twenty-two questions:

1. Why do Mark (8:27-30) and Luke (9:18-21), while they also recount the Caesarea Philippi conversation between Jesus and Peter, omit all reference to that part of Jesus' conversation which grants to Peter his alleged priority over the other apostles, the point which for Rome is the very heart and central point of our Lord's teaching ministry?

2. Why does the New Testament record more of Peter's errors after the Caesarea Philippi confession than of any of the other apostles? I am referring to (1) his "satanic" and "man-minding" rejection of Jesus' announcement that he would die, Matt 16:22-23; (2) his "leveling," or "Arian," comparison of Jesus with Moses and Elijah on the Mount of Transfiguration, Matt 17:4-5; (3) his ignorant and impetuous refusal to let Jesus wash his feet and then his self-willed dictating of the terms according to which Jesus would wash him, John 13:8-9; (4) his sleepiness while Jesus prayed in Gethsemane, Matt 26:36-45; (5) his precipitous use of the sword, Matt 26:51-54; (6) his prideful protestation of unfailing faithfulness and then his three denials of Jesus, recorded in all four Gospels; (7) his impulsive curiosity about John's future, expressed no sooner than Jesus had restored him to fellowship, which netted him Christ's stern "That's none of your business," John 21:21-22; and finally (8), even after Christ's resurrection, the Spirit's outpouring at Pentecost, and the role that he himself played in the Cornelius incident, his betrayal of the truth of the gospel of pure grace at Antioch by his compromising action which called for Paul's public rebuke in which Paul condemned him because "he was afraid of those who belonged to the circumcision group," because his action led the other Jewish Christians at Antioch, including even

Barnabas, to join him in his "hypocrisy," and, most significantly, because he was "not acting in line with the truth of the gospel" (Gal 2:11-14).

Where is the guarantee of the purity and continuity of the gospel in this man's actions?[30] It will not do to assert, as Origen, Chrysostom, and Jerome did, that Paul did not really rebuke Peter, that, rather, the two apostles simply arranged the whole event that Paul might the more effectively condemn the Judaizers. This explanation casts the shadow of dishonesty across the characters of both Peter and Paul. Nor will it do to declare as did Clement of Alexandria and some Jesuits later that it was not Peter the apostle but another Peter, one of the seventy, that Paul rebuked. Such an assertion needs no response; it is absurd since the context will not allow it. Nor does it satisfy matters simply to say that these errors on Peter's part only highlight the real oneness of the man with sinful humanity at large. For "actions speak louder than words," and in the last cited instance Peter's action, which alnost certainly was accompanied by some word of explanation from him to the church at Antioch in defense of his action, according to Paul, betrayed the purity of the gospel of grace as expressed in the foundational doctrine of justification by faith alone apart from works of law, which action on Peter's part both demanded and warranted Paul's public rebuke.[31]

---

[30] As an apostle of Christ, Peter's words were infallible when, and only when, under the Spirit's guidance, he spoke as an authoritative teacher of doctrine (1 Cor 2:13; 1 Thes 2:13; 2 Thes 2:15; 2 Cor 13:10; 1 John 4:6) and when he wrote his inerrant Spirit-inspired letters, 1 and 2 Peter (2 Peter 1:20-21). His actions were obviously not infallible here. In fact, his actions, doubtless accompanied by a word of explanation to someone for his actions, were not according to the truth of the gospel (Gal 2:14) and were therefore leading the church astray.

[31] The reader would be well advised to read in this connection Anglican Bishop J. C. Ryle's chapter on the "The Fallibility of Ministers" in his

3. Why can the disciples after the Caesarea Philippi incident still dispute among themselves concerning who was the greatest (Matt 18:1; 20:20-28; Luke 22:24)? Apparently *they* did not understand that Jesus' statement had given Peter any priority over them. And if Christ had in fact intended by his Caesarea Philippi pronouncement that Peter was to be his "vicar" and the leader of all Christendom, why did he not clear up the disciples' confusion once and for all by telling them so straightforwardly?

4. Why was Peter, if he was the head of the church, instead of sending other apostles to investigate the Samaritan revival, dispatched by the leaders of the Jerusalem church to investigate what was going on in Samaria (Acts 8:14)?

5. Why did the other apostles and the brotherhood in general feel they could challenge Peter's involvement in the Cornelius incident if he was in fact the undisputed and infallible head of the church (Acts 11:1-18)?

6. Why does Paul list Peter as only one of the "pillars" in Jerusalem, and second after James at that (Gal 2:9). And in this connection, why at the Jerusalem Council in Acts 15, over which James quite obviously presided, is Peter merely the first speaker, assuming no special prerogatives in the debate that ensued, and not the president of that Council? Why was the entire matter not simply submitted to Peter rather than to the Council, and why did not the decision go forth as a "Petrine" deliverance rather than an "apostolic" decree?

7. How can Paul say of the Jerusalem leadership (James, Peter and John) who "seemed to be something" (Gal 2:2, 6,

---

Warnings to the Churches (Reprint; Edinburgh: Banner of Truth, 1992), 93-121.

9), if Peter was the Christ-appointed leader of the church: "What they were makes no difference to me; *God shows no partiality*" (2:6)?

8. How can Rome escape Paul's implicit charge of creating a "Corinthian faction" disruptive to church unity (1 Cor 1:10-13; 3:3-9) when it urges the "primacy" of Peter over Paul, Apollos, and the universal church?

9. Why, if Peter was the bishop and pastor of Rome, as the Roman church maintains, and if it was Paul's established missionary practice "to preach the gospel where Christ was not known, so that I would not be building on someone else's foundation" (Rom 15:20; see 2 Cor 10:16),—why, I ask, does Paul declare that he had longed to come to Rome and had purposed many times to come there (but had been prevented before from doing so) "so that I may impart to you some spiritual gift to make you strong" and "in order that I might have a harvest among you, just as I have had among the other Gentiles" (Rom 1:11-13). Would not such activity at Rome on Paul's part have been both a denial of his own missionary policy and an affront to Peter whom Rome alleges was pastor there at that time?

10. Why does Peter describe himself as simply "*an* apostle of Jesus Christ," as one among many "living stones" (λίθοι ζῶντες, *lithoi zōntes*), and "the *fellow* elder" (ὁ συμπρεσ-βύτερος, *ho sumpresbuteros*), with other elders (1 Pet 1:1; 5:1)?

11. Why does Peter, if he was Rome's "first pope," contradict medieval Roman Catholic teaching that the purchase of indulgences will bring forgiveness of sin for oneself and will deliver one's loved ones from purgatory when he declared that "it was not with perishable things such as silver

and gold that you were redeemed...but with the precious blood of Christ" (1 Pet 1:18-19)?

12. Why does Peter, if he was Rome's "first pope," teach, *contra* Rome's teaching that the laity needs a priestly clergy to mediate between them and God, that in Christ all his readers are "a holy priesthood" (1 Pet 2:5, ἱεράτευμα ἅγιον, *hierateuma hagion*) and "a royal priesthood" (1 Pet 2:9, βασίλειον ἱεράτευμα, *basileion hierateuma*) who have direct access to God through Christ?

13. Why does Peter, if he was Rome's "first pope," teach, *contra* Rome's teaching, that the authority of the emperor, not the pope's, is "supreme" (ὑπερέχοντι, *huperechonti*) in secular matters (1 Pet 2:13)?

14. Why does Peter, if he was Rome's "first pope," teach, *contra* Rome's teaching, that Christians do not need to go to God through the mediation of Mary or any other saint since God gladly hears the prayers of his true children when they pray: "The eyes of the Lord are on the righteous, and his ears are attentive to their prayers" (1 Pet 3:12)?

15. Why does Peter, if he was Rome's "first pope," teach, *contra* Rome's teaching concerning the Mass as a necessary and essential 'unbloody' *sacrifice* of Christ, that Christ "died for sins *once for all* [ἅπαξ, *hapax*], the righteous for the unrighteous, to bring you to God" (1 Pet 3:18)?

16. Why, if Peter was the living, earthly head of the church at that time, does he disappear completely from Luke's Acts after Acts 15, with very few references to him, apart from his own two letters, in the rest of the New Testament?

17. Why in the earliest Patristic literature is Paul venerated as often as Peter, a fact admitted by Roman Catholic scholars?

18. Would John the "beloved disciple" and one of the original apostles, who apparently outlived Peter, have been subject to the bishop of Rome (Linus or Clement?) who succeeded to Peter's "throne"?

19. Why did no Roman bishop before Callistus I (d. c. 223 A.D.), who was sympathetic with modalism, though not uncritically so, use the Matthew 16 passage to support the primacy of the Roman bishopric; and when he did, why was he rebuked by such a notable contemporary as Tertullian who totally rejected the notion that Jesus' saying applied to later bishops at all? And Firmilian, bishop of Caesarea in Cappadocia, opposed the notion that the Roman bishopric is entitled by succession to the "throne" of Peter.

20. This raises the larger question, namely, while the church at Rome was no doubt influential,[32] why is there no indication in the first several centuries of the Christian era that any section of the church recognized the Roman church as supreme or that the rest of the church acceded to Rome any

---

[32] John Calvin (*Institutes*, 4.6.16) offered the following three reasons for the Roman church's early prestige: 1. The opinion became quite prevalent that Peter had founded and shepherded the church at Rome (this opinion was surely in error—RLR). 2. Because Rome was the capital city of the Empire, the church's leaders were probably more knowledgeable, skilled, and experienced than other church leaders in ecclesiastical matters (this is a *non sequitur*—RLR). 3. Because the Western half of the church was not as troubled by doctrinal controversy as the Eastern half, this added to Rome's authority as bishops deposed from their offices in the East, Greece, and Africa often sought both haven in Rome and the Roman bishop's endorsement of their cause.

claimed or recognized sovereignty over Christendom? And the Eastern church has never acceded this to Rome. [33]

21. Why did the first four ecumenical councils, which were held—two in the fourth, and two in the fifth century (whose doctrinal decisions are generally admitted by all Christians everywhere, including Protestants, to have been essentially orthodox)—neither say nor do anything which affords the slightest endorsement of the claim of the Roman bishop's supremacy but to the contrary in several instances actually passed decrees or canons which the bishop of Rome (or his agents) opposed and protested against, with the first such council which explicitly asserts the Roman bishop's supremacy being the Fourth Lateran Council held under Pope Innocent III in 1215 A.D.?

22. How does Roman Catholic theology in this entire matter avoid the charge of "asserting the consequence" or of "reasoning in a circle" (*petitio principii*) when it makes a highly questionable dogma (based as it is upon exegesis which has been approved by only a small minority of Fathers in the church), namely, its self-serving dogma of the primacy of the Roman bishop, the basis for its claim that it alone is justified in proclaiming any dogma whatsoever, including the Roman bishop's primacy over the entire church?

Needless to say, in my opinion Rome's exegesis of Matthew 16 and its developed dogmatic claim to papal authoritative primacy in the Christian church simply cannot be exegetically demonstrated and sustained from Scripture itself.

---

[33] The Roman Catholic apologist H. Burn-Murdock admits as much in his *The Development of the Papacy* (London: Faber & Faber, 1954), 130f., when he writes: "None of the writings of the first two centuries describe St. Peter as a bishop of Rome."

Moreover, its claim of papal supremacy is also a blatant rejection of many significant opposing testimonies in church history. While Jesus, true enough, said that upon "this rock" (ταύτῃ τῇ πέτρᾳ, *tautē tē petra*) he was going to build his "assembly," whether this phrase has for its antecedent Peter personally and exclusively and in what sense he was going to build his "assembly" on Peter have been matters of considerable controversy in the church from the beginning. Roman Catholic Archbishop Peter Richard Kenrick prepared a paper to be delivered at Vatican I (1870), in which he noted that five interpretations of the word "rock" were held in antiquity: (1) The first declared that the church was built on Peter, endorsed by seventeen Fathers. (2) The second understood the words as referring to all the apostles, Peter being simply the Primate, the opinion of eight Fathers. (3) The third asserted that the words applied to the faith which Peter professed, espoused by forty-four Fathers some of whom are the most important and representative. (4) The fourth declared that the words were to be understood of Jesus Christ, the church being built upon him, the view of sixteen Fathers. (5) The fifth understood the term "rock" to apply to the faithful themselves who, by believing in Christ, were made the living stones in the temple of his body, an opinion held by only very few.[34] These statistics show that the view that Vatican I eventually declared normative was a minority view in the ancient church, being held by about 20% of the Fathers consulted, and thus was far from certain. Where is Rome's allegiance to *this* ancient majority church tradition?

---

[34] Kenrick's paper was not permitted to be delivered at the Council but it was published later, along with other insights, under the title, *An Inside View of the Vatican Council*, ed. Leonard Woolsey Bacon (New York: American Tract Society, 1871). See particularly 107-8 for his findings on this matter. See also W. H. Griffith Thomas, *The Principles of Theology* (London: Longmans, Green, 1930), 470-1.

It obviously does not suit Rome's purpose to follow ancient church tradition here.

As samplings of this divergence of ancient opinion, *Origen*, making his usual distinction between the letter and the spiritual intention of the text, urged that according to the letter the rock in Jesus' explanation referred to Peter while the Spirit had in mind everyone who becomes such as Peter was.[35] *Tertullian* explicitly declared that the power to bind and to loose was given to Peter *personally* then and there and was not passed on to the Roman bishop.[36] *Cyprian* held that Jesus was addressing the whole body of bishops in speaking of Peter since, he says, he later endowed all the apostles "with a like partnership both of honour and power." He also contends that Jesus spoke specifically of Peter only to highlight the necessity of the *unity* of the church.[37] *Chrysostom*, followed by *Gregory of Nyssa, Isidore of Pelusium*, the Latin Father *Hilary*, and the later Greek Fathers *Theodoret, Theophanes, Theophylact*, and *John of Damascus*, held that the "rock" in Jesus' explanation was the faith of Peter's confession. The later *Augustine* believed that the rock was not Peter but Christ himself.[38]

---

[35] Origen, on Matt 16:18: "...rock means every disciple of Christ."

[36] Tertullian, *On Modesty*, xxi.

[37] Cyprian, *To the Lapsed*, Epistle XXVI.1; *On the Unity of the Church*, Treatise 1.4.

[38] Augustine, *Exposition on Psalm 61*, para. 3: "But in order that the Church might be built upon the Rock, who was made the Rock? Hear Paul saying: 'But the Rock was Christ.' On Him therefore built we have been"; *Sermon 26 on New Testament Lessons*, para. 1: "For seeing that Christ is the Rock (Petra), Peter is the Christian people.... [Christ said,] '...upon this Rock which thou hast confessed, upon this Rock which thou hast acknowledged, saying, 'Thou art the Christ, the Son of the living God,' will I build My Church, that is upon Myself, the Son of the living God, 'will I build My Church.' I will build thee upon Myself, not Myself upon thee." Para. 2: "Peter [was] built upon the Rock, not the Rock upon Peter." See also *On the Trinity*, II.17.28.

During the Middle Ages the Roman bishop regularly employed the passage to ground Rome's claim to ecclesiastical primacy as though no other understanding were possible. But at the time of the Reformation *Luther* returned to Augustine at this point ("The rock is the Son of God, Jesus Christ himself and no one else"), and urged that Peter's "rock-like" characteristic applied not to his person but only to his faith in Jesus who was the Rock.[39] *Calvin* also held that the Rock was Christ and that in addressing Peter as "Rock" Christ was addressing both Peter and all other believers as well in the sense that the bond of faith in Christ is the basis on which the church grows.[40] *Zwingli* taught that Peter is only the type of him who believes in Christ as the sole Rock.[41] It can be safely said, I think, that all of the Reformers believed that the true Rock of the church is Jesus Christ, with Peter being the "Rock" not in respect to his person but in respect to his being the type of all who trust in and confess Jesus as Messiah and God as he did.

---

[39] Martin Luther, *What Luther Says* (Saint Louis: Concordia, 1959), II, 1070, para. 3412: "The pope is the archblasphemer of God in that he applies to himself the noble passage which is spoken of Christ alone. He wants to be the rock, and the church should rest on him...Therefore we must see to it that we stay with the simple meaning, namely, that Christ is the Foundation on which the church is to stand." See Luther's *Works*, 17.II.449f.

[40] John Calvin, on Matthew 16:18; *Institutes*, 4.6.6.

[41] Ulrich Zwingli, "On the Lord's Supper," *Zwingli and Bullinger*, Vol. XXIV of the Library of Christian Classics (Philadelphia: Westminster, 1953), 192-3: "The papists might complain that we do not abide by the natural sense when it is a matter of the saying: 'Thou art Peter, that is, a stone, or rock, and upon this rock I will build my church.' Does that mean that we fall into error if we do not abide by the simple or natural sense...? Not at all. For we find that Christ alone is the rock, Christ alone is the Head, Christ alone is the vine in which we are held secure. Therefore Christ himself is the rock upon which the Church is built, and that is the natural sense of the words. As applied to the papacy, the words are not natural."

Given this divergence of opinion, what then *did* Jesus mean by his statement? I have argued in my *Jesus, Divine Messiah: the New Testament Witness* for the authenticity of the Matthean pericope. I argued in the same work that by his confession Peter declared his conviction that Jesus was both the long-promised Old Testament Messiah and the divine Son of God.[42] I pointed out there that it was in response to Peter's exclamatory declaration, "You are [σὺ εἶ, *su ei*] the Messiah, the Son of the living God!" that Jesus responded to Peter as he did: "And I am saying to you that you are [σὺ εἶ, *su ei*] a "peter" [lit., 'a rock']!" I think it important to note that in his exclamation Peter did not employ a proper name to designate Jesus; rather, he ascribed to him two titles, the first functional (Messiah), the second ontological (Son of the living God). I would suggest from the parallelism in the two σὺ εἶ (*su ei*) clauses that Jesus may have intended to respond in kind. That is to say, he may not have employed Πέτρος (*Petros*) as a proper name. Rather, he may have likewise ascribed to him only a title: "You are a rock [כֵּיפָא, *kêphā*]." And by capitalizing the Greek word Πέτρος (*Petros*) as it does, the Greek rendering of the Aramaic כֵּיפָא (*kêphā*) which latter word Jesus almost certainly used, the editors of our critical editions of the Greek New Testament may have misled us. Jesus may have intended to say, in other words, not "You are Peter," but "You are a rock!" by which exclamation I suggest he would have meant, "You are [truly] a rock [by describing me as you just did]!" If so, when Jesus continued by saying, "and upon *this rock* [note: he does not say "upon *you*"[43]] I will build my 'assembly,'" I would suggest

---

[42] See my *Jesus, Divine Messiah: The New Testament Witness* (Phillipsburg, N. J.: Presbyterian and Reformed, 1990), 50-1, 176-8.

[43] If Christ had meant by his expression "this rock" the man Peter, why did he not say: "upon *you* I will build my church," as plainly as he said: "to you I will give the keys"?

that he intended to say that it was upon Peter's "rock-like" *description* of him as the Messiah and the Son of the living God, *which understanding the Father had just graciously revealed to him*, and not upon Peter *personally* that he would ground his church. This would mean, in sum, that the "bedrock" itself of the church is the fact of Christ's own messianic investiture and his ontological existence as the Second Person of the Godhead, just as Paul would later write: "No man can lay a foundation other than the one which is laid, which is Jesus Christ" (1 Cor 3:11; see also 1 Cor 10:4: "...and the rock was Christ [ἡ πέτρα δὲ ἦν ὁ Χριστός, *hē petra de ēn ho Christos*]"). In confessing the same Peter was himself "a rock."

It is just possible, of course, that Jesus did intend to say that upon Peter he would build his church *in some sense* (I think sometimes that our "Protestant" reluctance to admit this possibility plays into the hands of the Roman apologist), a possibility that receives some support from the next verse where Jesus declared to Peter: "I will give to *you* [sing.] the keys of the kingdom of heaven,[44] and whatever *you* [sing.] bind upon earth shall have been bound in heaven, and whatever

---

[44] This phrase, "the keys of the kingdom of heaven," of course, symbolically denotes kingdom authority, so Jesus in Matthew 16 is granting "kingdom-building authority" to Peter. But this authority must not be interpreted one-sidedly—as is occasionally done because of the Matthew 18 context—as having reference only to church discipline. The phrase in Matthew 16 follows upon Jesus' positive declaration that he would "build" his church. Moreover, Jesus declares that by these keys Peter would both bind *and* loose. Therefore, the authority to open or close the doors of the kingdom of heaven to men which Jesus grants to Peter here (and to the other original disciples in Matthew 18:18) must be seen to include both the authority to proclaim the liberating gospel and the authority to take disciplinary steps to exclude the impenitent sinner in order to insure that the church remains pure. By means of both Jesus would "build" his "assembly." There is a polemical side to

you [sing.] loose upon earth shall have been loosed in heaven"
(16:19).[45] But in what sense did he intend this?

Peter's confession of Jesus as Messiah and Son of the
living God, just revealed to him by the Father, cannot and
must not be excluded from Christ's reference to Peter as "a
rock." That is to say, not Peter personally but *Peter as the
confessing apostle*—confessing what he did, namely, the
revealed truth about Jesus being the Messiah and the Son of

---

our Lord's statement here as well, for in giving this "kingdom-building
authority" to his church, he was saying not the ordained rabbis who "sit
in Moses' seat," who neither had entered the kingdom themselves nor
were aiding others to enter, but his confessing "assembly" possess "the
keys of knowledge" (Luke 11:52).

Geerhardus Vos, professor of biblical theology at Princeton Seminary,
argues in his *The Teaching of Jesus Concerning the Kingdom of God
and the Church* (Nutley, N. J., Presbyterian and Reformed, 1972 reprint),
81, that the authority to bind and to loose goes beyond the authority to
impute and to forgive sin and refers to "the administration of the affairs
of the house [of God] in general." When one takes into account that this
authority was also given to the other apostles and that their doctrinal
teaching became the foundation of the church (Eph 2:20), Vos' broader
construction of Jesus' intent is entirely possible.

[45] The "shall have been bound" and the "shall have been loosed" in
my translation of the Greek text of Matthew 16:19 (and 18:18) reflect
the fact that underlying both is a verbal construction known as the
future perfect passive periphrastic. Henry J. Cadbury in "The Meaning
of John 20[23], Matthew 16[19], and Matthew 18[18]," *JBL* (Vol 58, Sept
1939), 253, urges that "the simple future seems...as adequate as any
English translation can be" for this Greek construction. But J. R. Mantey,
both in "The Mistranslation of the Perfect Tense in John 20[23], Mt 16[19],
and Mt 18[18]" in the same journal issue and in "Evidence That the Perfect
Tense in John 20:23 and Matthew 16:19 Is Mistranslated," *JETS* (Vol
16, No 3, Summer 1973), 129-38, demonstrates that the translations I
have urged above are not only warranted but also really the only English
translations which capture the force of the Greek. Thus if the binding
and loosing about which Jesus speaks here pertain respectively to
"retaining" and "forgiving" men's sins (see John 20:23; see Rev 1:5),
this can only mean, in my opinion, that those whom the church through

the living God—is the foundation rock of the church. Edmund P. Clowney, professor emeritus of practical theology, Westminster Seminary, explains why this must be so:

> This interpretation is demanded by the sequel in the passage which follows (Mt. 16:22-23). There Jesus calls Peter by another name: Satan. Just as Peter had spoken by revelation from the Father, he now becomes the

---

the proclamation of the gospel brings to faith are those who are already God's elect and those who finally spurn the church's message or who are finally excommunicated by the church are those who are already the non-elect.

D. A. Carson in his *Matthew* in *The Expositor's Bible Commentary* (Grand Rapids: Zondervan, 1984), 8, 373, agrees with my translation of the Greek construction but his understanding of the significance of this translation differs from mine: "Whatever [Peter] binds or looses will have been bound or loosed, so long as he adheres to that divinely disclosed gospel…Those he ushers in or excludes have already been bound or loosed by God according to the gospel already revealed…." In my opinion, Carson's explanation of the meaning of the text is not very helpful.

One final comment is in order: Jesus was not instituting the current Roman Catholic priestly practice of absolution when he granted to the original disciples the authority to "bind" or "loose" men's sins. If he was, we must conclude that the disciples just did not get it, for nowhere in Acts or in the New Testament epistles do we find them hearing confessions and absolving the penitent of their sins by requiring of them acts of penance. What we do see them doing is preaching the gospel and disciplining the backslidden Christian. Nor was Jesus instituting the priestly practice of absolution in John 20:22, as Rome contends (*Catechism of the Catholic Church*, para. 976): (1) the verb, "he breathed," is aoristic and has no specified object, suggesting a *single* expulsion of breath upon *all* the disciples present, not just upon some individuals among them; (2) others, in addition to the apostles, were surely present; see Luke 24:33ff. This action on Jesus' part he intended as a depiction of his impending action on the Day of Pentecost; see Acts 1:5, 8; 2:2, 4, 33.

mouthpiece of the devil. In confessing Jesus to be the Christ he was the rock, in tempting Jesus to refuse the cross he is Satan. He is called Satan only in direct reference to his word of seduction. Apart from that expression the designation does not apply. Jesus is not declaring that Peter the man is a Satan in terms of all his personal qualities, nor is satanicity a *character indelibilis*. Peter is Satan as he speaks for Satan. [This would require by analogy that we understand that] Peter is a rock as he speaks for God.[46]

This conclusively shows *exegetically* that Peter was "rock-like" *only* in his office as a confessing apostle speaking the Word of God. If and when he spoke something authoritatively other than the Word of God, he became instead of a foundational rock a "Satan" (may we even say an "Antichrist"?), instead of a foundational rock a "stumbling block" (σκάνδαλον, *skandalon*)!

It must be noted in this connection that to the rest of the disciples (Matt 18:1) several days later Jesus gave the same kingdom authority that he had given to Peter when he said, "Truly I say to *you* [pl.], whatever *you* [pl.] bind upon earth shall have been bound in heaven, and whatever *you* [pl.] loose upon earth shall have been loosed in heaven" (18:18). And he did the same thing on the night of his resurrection when he "breathed on [the ten disciples] and said, 'Receive the Holy Spirit. Whoever's sins *you* [pl.] forgive, they have been forgiven; whoever's *you* [pl.] retain, they have been retained'" (John 20:22-23). What should we make of this similar promise of the keys to the other disciples? I would contend that Jesus was inferring on these two latter occasions what Paul would later state explicitly, namely, that Christ's church

---

[46] E. P. Clowney, *The Biblical Doctrine of the Church* (unpublished classroom syllabus), II, 108-9.

would be "built on the foundation of the apostles and prophets, Christ Jesus himself being the cornerstone" (Eph 2:20; see 1 Cor 10:4), and what John would later symbolically depict in the Revelation as one aspect of the church as the "bride" of Christ: "...the wall of the city [the Lamb's wife, that is, his church] had twelve foundation stones, and on them were the twelve names of the twelve apostles of the Lamb" (Rev 21:14).

In sum, the totality of New Testament teaching, it seems quite clear, grants a certain priority to Peter among the original Twelve, but this priority, to use Jack Dean Kingsbury's phrase, seems to have been "salvation- [or redemptive-] historical" in nature, that is to say, Peter occupied a *primus inter pares* position only during the specific time frame of the "salvation history" in which he lived.[47] The New Testament does not restrict the church's foundation to him alone but founds the church on the entire apostolate, not in regard to their persons as such but in regard to their office in the church as authoritative teachers of doctrine who confess the truth about Jesus' deity and messiahship. I must conclude from all of the Scripture data that there is no warrant whatever in these words of Jesus for Rome's dogma of the exclusive primacy of "Peter's chair" within Christendom.

The Verdict of Church History on Rome's Papal Claims

Before I move to the second half of my answer, I should note that church history itself has something to say about Rome's claim of having an infallible papal head. First, with regard to the very election of popes, the *New Catholic Encyclopedia* acknowledges that

---

[47] Jack Dean Kingsbury, "The Figure of Peter in Matthew's Gospel as a Theological Problem," *JBL* 98/1 (March 1979), 67-83.

from the 4th to the 11th century the influence of temporal rulers in papal elections reached its zenith. Not only the Roman emperors but also, in their turn, the Ostrogoth kings of Italy [who were Arians—RLR] and the Carolingian emperors attempted to control the selection of the Roman pontiff. This civil intervention ranged from the approval of elected candidates to the actual nomination of candidates (with tremendous pressure exerted on the electors to secure their acceptance), and even to the extreme of forcible deposition and imposition.[48]

This acknowledgement simply means, according to the stated stipulations of Rome's own canon law, that many of the papal elections were corrupted and thus invalidated by secular political forces.

If this were not problem enough for papal claims to infallibility, when one notes that, according to the *New Catholic Encyclopedia*, the sacrament of holy orders requires in the one receiving the sacrament (and surely this would include papal electors and the pope himself) "outstanding and habitual goodness of life, especially *perfect* chastity,"[49] it is apparent, first, that a papal election would be invalid if the margin of votes that effected his election were cast by those whose own ordinations were invalid because of the absence of this condition of "outstanding and

---

[48] A. Swift, "Popes, Election of," *New Catholic Encyclopedia* (New York: McGraw-Hill, 1967), 11.572b.

[49] N. Halligan, "Holy Orders," *New Catholic Encyclopedia*, 7.89a (emphasis supplied). But when S. O'Riordan, "Chastity," in the *New Catholic Encyclopedia* states: "Mere conscious rejection or *unconscious* repression of sexuality is not chastity, for neither constitutes a moral moderation of sexuality but only warps and frustrates it" (3.516a, emphasis supplied), this definition alone makes it impossible for the Roman Church ever to know whether anyone receiving Holy Orders possesses the requisite conditions for the priesthood.

habitual goodness" and "perfect chastity" within them. Second, when one then takes into account that, according to Holy Scripture, no priest (except One, even Jesus Christ!) has ever possessed this condition, one must acknowledge that the problem of knowing for certain that a given pope's election is valid ceases to be simply a theoretical one. In fact, the *certain* validity of any pope's election rises to the level of an impossibility!

Second, in its entry, "Antipope," the *New Catholic Encyclopedia* acknowledges: "...it must be frankly admitted that bias or deficiencies in the sources makes it impossible to determine in certain cases whether the claimants [to the papal throne] were popes or antipopes."[50] This is quite an admission! While I cannot provide in this short monograph a detailed account of these cases of papal conflict, the following two segments of papal history illustrate the hopelessness of Rome's ever knowing for certain whether any modern pope is the true successor to Peter.

During the fourteenth and fifteenth centuries (1378-1409) a series of rival Antipopes, each with his college of cardinals, resided simultaneously at Rome (Urban VI, Boniface IX, Innocent VII, Gregory XII) and at Avignon in France (Clement VII, Benedict XIII), each claiming to be Peter's legitimate heir, with each rival "fulminating the severest judgments of heaven against each other" (Schaff) and excommunicating the other. Accordingly, the church was divided between these papal "obediences," with France, Scotland, Savoy, Lorraine, Castile, Aragon, and parts of Germany acknowledging the Avignon popes and Italy, England, other parts of Germany, Sweden, Poland, and Hungary acknowledging the Roman popes. In 1409 a council convened at Pisa and, asserting the conciliar principle that an ecumenical council is superior to a pope, declared both Gregory XII and Benedict XIII to

---

[50] H. G. J. Beck, "Antipope," *New Catholic Encyclopedia* , 1.632a.

be "notorious schismatics, promoters of schism, and notorious heretics, errant from the faith, and guilty of the notorious and enormous crimes of perjury and violated oaths" and proceeded to elect its own pope, Alexander V, who was almost immediately followed by John XXIII. Now there were three popes, each claiming papal legitimacy! This papal schism, known by church historians as the "Great Schism," was finally brought to an end in 1417 by the Council of Constance[51] where Gregory XII resigned, provided that Benedict XIII and John XXIII would also be set aside. The council did indeed depose Benedict XIII and John XXIII, the latter of whom was tried on seventy charges which included almost every crime known to man.[52] The Council then elected Martin V whose papal line is accepted by the Roman Church today as the legitimate papal line.[53] The point in my recounting this bit of papal history is simply to highlight for the reader the fact that Rome can never be sure

---

[51] This same council also prevailed upon Sigismund, king of the Romans, to retract his promise of safe-conduct to the pre-reformer John Hus who had come to the council to defend his advocacy of Wycliff's teachings and turned him over to the civil authority to be burned at the stake. His martyrdom took place July 6, 1415.

[52] When Angelo Cardinal Roncalli was elected pope in 1958 he chose for his papal title the name of John XXIII, thereby formally branding the medieval pope John XXIII as an Antipope and also thereby effectively erasing him from Catholic papal history. But by doing so Cardinal Roncalli's choice of papal titles by implication recognized both the Council of Constance as an ecumenical council and the conciliar principle that it espoused in its fourth and fifth sessions to the effect that an ecumenical council's authority is superior to that of the pope, a principle which all modern popes reject.

[53] Even though the decrees of the Council of Constance's fourth and fifth sessions declared that the authority of an ecumenical council is superior to that of the pope that it elected and the subsequent line of popes that Rome recognizes today, the validity of the conciliar principle was officially set aside again by Vatican I in 1870.

that its present pope is indeed the direct successor of Peter in a succession that has experienced no intervening nullifying breach of apostolic succession. All Rome can do is assert that he is, undergirding its assertion with casuistical arguments which are contradicted by formal statements made by Martin V himself who necessarily had to accept the superiority and authority of ecumenical councils over popes in order to justify his own election.[54]

A little over two decades later, on June 25, 1439 the Council of Basel (1431-49), duly appointed by both Pope Martin V and his successor Pope Eugenius IV, "deposed, deprived, and cast down" Eugenius as a disturber of the peace of the church, a simoniac and perjurer, incorrigible and errant from the faith, and a schismatic and a pertinacious heretic, together with the whole company of cardinals and bishops who had plotted the dissolution of the council with him, and on November 5 of that same year the council elected in his place Amadeus VIII, Duke of Savoy, who, with the support of Savoy, some of the German princes, Alfonso of Aragon, and the universities of Paris, Vienna, Cologne, Erfurt, and Cracow, assumed the papal office on January 1, 1440 as Felix V. Eugenius, however, refused to recognize the council's act of deposition, even though in a decree issued on December 13, 1433 he himself had pronounced and declared the

---

[54] Because the Council of Constance meets none of Rome's current conditions for being an ecumenical council (see F. J. Murphy, "Councils, Canon Law of," *New Catholic Encyclopedia*, 4.373a), Rome has always left its "canonical status" somewhat unclear for it confronts the Roman papacy with an indissoluble dilemma: This council cannot be formally ratified without affirming the primacy of councils over popes, but it cannot be dismissed either without reopening the entire debate that raged at the time of the Great Schism. See Philip Schaff, *History of the Christian Church* (Reprint; Grand Rapids: Eerdmans, 1963), VI, 165-6, for his assessment of Rome's arguments for Martin's legitimacy and his refutation of them.

"General Council of Basel legitimate from the time of its opening," and curried the favor and eventually won the support of the new emperor, Frederick III. Whereupon, Felix issued a bull anathematizing Eugenius. So once again the church experienced papal schism with two men claiming to be the legitimate pope, both having been elected by actions of duly constituted councils. But through political intrigue and unkept promises on Eugenius's part to recognize the superiority of general councils, he was able to retain his hold on the Roman see. Consequently, on April 7, 1449 Felix revoked his anathema and abdicated, having been appeased by the cardinal's cap of Sabina and the Apostolic vicarage of Savoy and other regions which had recognized his "obedience." What we have here is the election of a pope (Felix), duly solemnized by the authority of a general council that was convoked by not one but two papal bulls and consecrated by the presiding legate of the Roman see, overturned by the recalcitrance of a dishonest claimant to the papal throne. But then, as John Calvin notes: "From these rebellious and obstinate heretics [Eugenius and his supporters] have come forth all future popes, cardinals, bishops, abbots, and priests."[55]

No one should question the historical accuracy of my depiction or interpretation of these segments of papal history, for no less a Roman Catholic authority than Joseph Cardinal Ratzinger, current head of the Sacred Congregation of the Doctrine of the Faith for the Church of Rome, has observed about this bizarre segment of church history:

> For nearly half a century, the Church was split into two or three obediences that excommunicated one another, so

---

[55] John Calvin, "Prefatory Address to King Francis I of France," *Institutes of the Christian Religion*, translated by Ford Lewis Battles (Philadelphia: Westminster, 1960), 27.

that every Catholic lived under excommunication by one pope or another, and, *in the last analysis, no one could say with certainty which of the contenders had right on his side.* The Church no longer offered certainty of salvation; she had become questionable in her whole objective form—the true Church, the true pledge of salvation, had to be sought outside the institution. It is against this background of a profoundly shaken ecclesial consciousness that we are to understand that Luther, in the conflict between his search for salvation and the tradition of the Church, ultimately came to experience the Church, not as the guarantor, but as the adversary of salvation.[56]

Moreover, with regard to the Roman church's Vatican I declaration of infallibility for the Roman papacy (1870)—which declaration has contributed in a major way to ongoing schism within Christendom—not only has all the rest of Christendom, Orthodox and Protestant alike, formally and officially rejected it[57] but also even many thoughtful Roman Catholic scholars have refused to accept it. For example, one of the greatest Roman Catholic historians of the nineteenth century, John Emerich Edward Dalberg, better known to the world as Lord Acton[58] who coined the warning: "Power tends to corrupt; absolute power corrupts absolutely"

---

[56] Joseph Cardinal Ratzinger, *Principles of Catholic Theology*, translated by Sister Mary Frances McCarthy (San Francisco: Ignatius, 1989), 196, emphasis supplied.

[57] I would refer the student who is interested in reading more about this matter to William Cunningham's brilliant treatment, "The Papal Supremacy," *Historical Theology* (Edinburgh: Banner of Truth, 1960 reprint), I, 207-26.

[58] I am indebted to John W. Robbins' *Ecclesiastical Megalomania* for calling my attention to the cited statements of Lord Acton and Ignaz von Döllinger.

(it is not commonly known by those who are familiar with his warning that Lord Acton was directing it not only against kings but also against the papacy), published an essay three years before Vatican I in which he warned the Roman Church of the consequences of the dogma of papal infallibility:

It is more profitable [he noted] to study the consequences than to estimate the chances of success [of a Council's issuing a decree of papal infallibility]. A decree proclaiming the Pope infallible would be a confession that the authority of General Councils has been an illusion and a virtual usurpation from the first; so that having come to the knowledge of their own superfluousness, and having directed the Church into the way she ought always to have followed, they could only abolish themselves for the future by an act of suicide. It would invest, by its retrospective action, not the Pope and his successors only, but all his legitimate predecessors, with the same immunity. The objects of faith would be so vastly increased by the incorporation of the [papal] Bullarium, that the limits would become indistinct by distance. The responsibility for the acts of the buried and repented past would come back at once and forever, with a crushing weight on the Church. Specters it has taken ages of sorrowful effort to lay [aside] would come forth once more. The Bulls...which prescribed the tortures and kindled the flames of the Inquisition, the Bulls which erected witchcraft into a system and made the extermination of witches a frightful reality, would become as venerable as the decrees of Nicaea, as incontrovertible as the writing of S. Luke. The decision of every tribunal (by the decretal *Novit*) would be made subject to the revision of the Pope, and the sentences of every Protestant judge (by the Bull *Cum ex apostolatus officio*) would be invalid. The priesthood would be, by Divine right, exempt from all secular allegiance; and the supreme authority over all States would revert to the Holy See—for thus it stands in the Bull *Unam Sanctam*, repeated by Leo X in the Fifth Council of Lateran. Catholics would be bound, by order of Innocent III, to obey all the laws of Deuteronomy. A successor of Alexander VI might distribute the New World over again; and the right by which Adrian disposed of Ireland would enable another Pope to barter it for a Concordat with America, or to exchange Great Britain for a French garrison...The church would take the place of the moon, reflecting passively the light which the Pope receives directly from Heaven, but liable to be left in total darkness, sometimes for three years together, during the vacancy of the Holy See, and during much longer periods of schism, when she knows not her rightful head. And as the Pope's decisions would be, not a testimony of the existing faith of the Church, but a result of his own enlightenment by the Holy Ghost, his interpretation and application of Scripture would be also infallible, the dogma could not be separated from the proofs, and the arguments of the mediaeval Bulls would become a norm for theology.... Rome has before now insisted on opinions which set a barrier to conversions and supplied a motive for persecution. The preservation of authority is a higher object than the propagation of the faith. The advocates of Roman views are more used to controversy with their fellow Catholics than with Protestants. Their first aspiration is to suppress divisions of opinion within the Church; and this object could not be achieved more effectually than by converting the Vatican into a sort of Catholic Delphi.[59]

---

[59] Lord Acton, "The Next General Council," *Chronicle*, July 13, 1867, 369-70, as cited by Hugh MacDougall, *The Acton-Newman Relations* (New York: Fordham University Press, 1962). No Protestant, unless it

Another example of the same rejection of papal infallibility may be cited. A year after Vatican I, in a letter to the Archbishop of Munich, the foremost Roman Catholic historian in Germany, Ignaz von Döllinger, denounced the Vatican Decrees:

---

be Martin Luther or John Calvin, has surpassed Lord Acton in the severity of his judgment of the papacy. As a historian Lord Acton carefully researched the Roman Inquisition and concluded:

> The object of the Inquisition [was] not to combat sin—for sin was not judged by it unless accompanied by [theological] error. Nor even to put down error. For it punished untimely and unseemly remarks the same as blasphemy. Only unity. This became an outward, fictitious, hypocritical unity. The gravest sin was pardoned, but it was death to deny the *Donation of Constantine*. So men learned that outward submission must be given. All this [was] to promote authority more than faith. When ideas were punished more severely than actions...—and the *Donation* was put on a level with God's own law— men understood that authority went before sincerity. (Acton, Add. MSS, 4939; as cited by Gertrude Himmelfarb, *Lord Acton: A Study in Conscience and Politics* [Chicago: University Press, 1952], 162)

In 1868 he published a long essay in the *North British Review* about the St. Bartholomew's Eve Massacres. In 1572 a large number of Huguenot (French Protestants) notables had come to Paris to attend the wedding of Henry of Navarre to the sister of King Charles IX. Catherine de Medici, the queen mother, conspired to have them killed. At the pre-established signal on August 24, Catholics roamed through the streets of Paris killing around 2000 Protestants and around 20,000 others in some other large French cities were also massacred. Hearing the news, Pope Gregory XIII rejoiced and ordered thanksgiving services and the ringing of church bells in all the churches. Lord Acton goes even further, declaring:

> The story is much more abominable than we all believed.... S.B. is the greatest crime of modern times. It was committed on principles professed by Rome. It was approved, sanctioned, and praised by the papacy. The Holy See went out of its way to signify to the world, by permanent and solemn acts, how entirely it admired a king

[The Pope's] authority is unlimited, incalculable; it can strike, as Innocent III says, wherever sin is; it can punish every one; it allows no appeal and is itself Sovereign Caprice; for the Pope carries, according to the expression

---

who slaughtered his subjects treacherously, because they were Protestants. To proclaim forever that because a man is a Protestant it is a pious deed to cut his throat in the night. (Lord Acton, Add. MSS 5004, cited by Himmelfarb, *Lord Acton*, 67)

Having carefully studied the history of the Roman church, Lord Acton concluded among other things that

the papacy contrived murder and massacred on the largest and also on the most cruel and inhuman scale. They [the Popes] were not only wholesale assassins but they made the principle of assassination a law of the Christian Church and a condition of salvation.... (Lord Acton, *Correspondence*, 55, cited by Himmelfarb, *Lord Acton*, 104)

The papacy sanctions murder; the avowed defender and promoter of the papacy is necessarily involved in that sanction.... No man defends the papacy who has not accommodated his conscience to the idea of assassination. (Cited by MacDougall, *The Acton-Newman Relations*, 142)

The reader should recall here, as Lord Acton pointed out, that if popes are infallible, then Rome's sanction of murder and assassination Rome must defend as correct and proper. Himmelfarb herself writes:

How the papacy lost its early innocence, degenerating into an absolute power, is the long and disreputable story of forgeries and fabrications, of which the *Donation of Constantine* in the eighth century and the *Isidorian Decretals* in the ninth were only the most flagrant episodes. Usurping the rights of the episcopacy and of the general councils, the papacy was finally driven to the principles and methods of the Inquisition to enforce its spurious claims and to the theory of infallibility to elevate it beyond all human control. [Döllinger in his *The Pope and the Council*] piled high the sordid details of inventions and distorted texts, of Popes involved in contradiction and heresy, of historians falsifying history and theologians perverting theology. (*Lord Acton*, 97)

of Boniface VIII, all rights in the Shrine of his breast. As he has now become infallible, he can by the use of the little word, "orbi,"...make every rule, every doctrine, every demand, into a certain and incontestable article of faith. No right can stand against him, no personal or corporate liberty; or as the Canonists puts it—"The tribunal of God and of the pope is one and the same." This system bears its Roman origin on its brow, and will never be able to force its way in German lands. As a Christian, as a Theologian, as a Reader of history, as a Citizen, I cannot accept this doctrine; for it is irreconcilable with the spirit of the Gospel, and with the clear declaration of Christ and the Apostles; it wishes directly to set up a kingdom of this world which Christ declined; it covets the Lordship over the Churches which Peter forbade to all and to himself. Not as a Theologian; for the whole, genuine tradition of the Church stands in irreconcilable opposition to it. Not as a Reader of history can I accept it; for as such, I know that the persistent striving to realize this theory of world domination, has cost Europe rivers of blood, has distracted and desolated whole countries, has torn to pieces the beautiful, organic constitution of the ancient Church, and has engendered, nourished, and maintained the worst of ecclesiastical abuses. Finally, as a Citizen, I must beckon it away from me; because by its claims to the prostration of the States and Monarchs and the whole political order of things under the authority of the Pope, and by the privileged position which it demands for the Clergy, it lays the foundation for an endless and destructive schism between the Church and State, between Cleric and Layman. For I cannot conceal from myself, that this Dogma...would, were it to become dominant in the Catholic section of the German nation, immediately also plant, in the new Empire, which has just been established, the germ of an incurable disorder.[60]

Lord Acton and Ignaz von Döllinger have been by no means the only Roman Catholics to criticize the papacy and its claims. Many another scholar has also. Dante, for instance, in the fourteenth century denounced in his *De Monarchia* the claims of the papacy as unscriptural, unhistorical, and illogical, and portrayed the papacy of Boniface VIII in his *The Divine Comedy, Paradiso*, xxvii, 40-60, as a "sewer of blood and stench."[61] In sum, this dogma of Rome regarding its "infallible Head"—as evidenced by Scripture, history, and right reason—is surely one of the greatest—if not *the* greatest—hoaxes foisted upon professing Christendom.[62]

---

[60] Ignaz von Döllinger, *A Letter Addressed to the Archbishop of Munich* (London: 1871), as cited by MacDougall, *The Acton-Newman Relations*, 119-20. See also his *The Pope and the Council* (Boston, 1870).

[61] For more examples of papal failings, one may consult J. N. D. Kelly, *The Oxford Dictionary of Popes* (Oxford: Oxford Press, 1986); R. McBrien, *Lives of the Popes* (HarperCollins, 1997); and B. J. Kidd, *The Roman Primacy to A.D. 461* (London: SPCK, 1936).

[62] The spurious *Donation of Constantine*, cited by no less than ten popes of whom we know in their claims of papal control over lands and monarchies, also played a role in establishing this hoax. (Since it was spurious, where is the infallibility of these popes?) This document, purportedly from the Emperor Constantine but shown by Nicholas of Cusa and Lorenzo Valla in the fifteenth century by means of careful textual criticism to have been drawn up most probably during the pontificate of Paul I (A.D. 757-767), cedes to Sylvester I (A.D. 314-335) primacy over Antioch, Constantinople, Alexandria, and Jerusalem, and dominion over all of Italy, including Rome, and the "provinces, places, and *civitates*" of the Western half of the Roman Empire. Christopher B. Coleman, *The Treatise of Lorenzo Valla on the Donation of Constantine* (New York: Russell and Russell, 1971 reprint of the 1922 edition), 7-8, writes:

The papacy was then cutting loose from the Emperor at Constantinople and ignoring his representatives in Italy, as well as developing its own independent policy toward Italian territory, toward the Lombards,

The upshot of all this—and this concludes the first half of my response to the class member's original question—is that Rome bases all of its teachings and actions, and this includes its soteriological teaching, not primarily on Scripture but primarily on its own "infallible, unamendable" Tradition. And this Tradition virtually from the beginning began to exhibit great error and has continued to exhibit greater and greater contradictions and inconsistencies throughout the centuries.

---

and toward the Franks. The aim of the forger seems to have been the characteristically medieval one of supplying documentary warrant for the existence of the situation which had developed through a long-drawn-out revolution, namely, the passage of imperial prerogatives and political control in Italy from the Emperor to the papacy.

This document, in a word, made the popes successors to the Roman Caesars, not to the apostle Peter, and thereby also Roman Emperors ruling over a vast empire. For nearly eight centuries the papacy traced its political power to this document until it was exposed as a forgery, probably committed by the papacy itself to bolster its pretensions to political power. Although the document's character as a forgery is not debated by present-day scholarship, after five hundred years these new Roman Caesars have yet to acknowledge that their claim to political power and jurisdiction during the Middle Ages, not to mention the actual political and economic advances which they achieved during that time, rested on a forgery (under pressure from Benito Mussolini the Vatican in 1929 did finally cede Italy's share of the "gift" back to Italy), doubtless because to do so would wreck the papal claim to both political power and infallibility and also because the papacy still entertains aspirations to rule the entire world not only religiously but also politically—"in the name of Christ," of course. Perhaps the Westminster divines were not wrong when they declared that the Roman papacy is not the head of the church but to the contrary is the Antichrist (*Westminster Confession of Faith*, XXV.vi).

For Valla's proofs that the *Donation* was a forgery, see Coleman, *The Treatise of Lorenzo Valla on the Donation of Constantine*.

The Apostate Character of Rome's Tradition Concerning Paul's Law-Free Gospel of Justification by Faith Alone

With this last observation we come to the second half of my response to the class member's original question, namely, that Rome's tradition, in which it places so much stock, has been by and large bad tradition.

The Apostolic Fathers and Their "Doctrinal Trajectory"

Paul's characterization of the Galatian churches—"you are so quickly deserting the one who called you in the grace of Christ" (1:6)—could quite appropriately be employed to describe the early church's doctrinal drift as a whole, for it is one of the saddest facts of church history that the post-apostolic church's soteriological deliverances quickly launched the church on a doctrinal trajectory in the area of soteriology that more and more moved virtually the entire church away from the pristine Pauline teaching on salvation by pure grace and justification by faith alone.[63] And I am not referring to the relatively insignificant kinds of errors that often occur when any uninspired theologian begins to comment upon the inspired Scriptures. I am talking about

---

[63] I do not intend to suggest for a moment by this remark that the church completely lost the gospel for 1,500 years or that no one after the Apostolic Age had a saving understanding of Paul's doctrine of justification by faith before the age of the Reformation. There was doubtless always a remnant of God's elect who understood Paul's gospel. And there was always what Albrecht Ritschl termed "the religious self-estimate" of godly men, such as Augustine, Bernard and Staupitz, who, while working within the forms of official theology of the church, yet acknowledged that all of God's saving benefits flow from grace.

serious doctrinal heresy. For from the Apostolic Fathers
onward the church fell more and more into serious
soteriological error, with grace and faith giving way to
legalism and the doing of good works as the pronounced
way of salvation. An unevangelical nomism runs virtually
unabated through the writings of these church fathers. Not
even fully in Augustine in the fifth century, and only upon
rare later occasion after him (for example, Gottschalk and
Bradwardine, Wycliffe and Hus), was the voice of Paul
clearly heard again before the sixteenth-century magisterial
Reformation where it was then heard in the powerful
preaching, teaching, and writing of Martin Luther and John
Calvin. Many authorities might be cited in support of this
general observation. The great—admittedly liberal—
Ritschlian church historian Adolf von Harnack who taught
at the University of Berlin from 1889 to 1921 in both his
History of Dogma and *Mission and Expansion of the
Church* contended that the Christianity of the second century
was a corrupt synthesis of Hellenism and the evangelical
religion of the apostolic age. In his famous quip he declared:
"Marcion was the only Gentile Christian who understood
Paul, and even he misunderstood him." Kenneth Escott Kirk,
Anglican bishop of Oxford, in his 1928 Bampton Lectures
observes that

> St. Paul's indignant wonder was evoked by the reversion
> of a small province of the Christian Church [Galatia] to
> the legalistic spirit of the Jewish religion. Had he lived
> half a century or a century later, his cause for amazement
> would have been increased a hundredfold. The example
> of the Galatians might be thought to have infected the
> entire Christian Church; writer after writer seems to have
> little other interest than to express the genius of
> Christianity wholly in terms of law and obedience, reward
> and punishment.[64]

Benjamin B. Warfield, professor of didactic and polemic theology at Princeton Seminary from 1887 to 1921—as orthodox as Harnack was liberal—observed in 1897: "There is a great gulf cleft between the writings of the apostles and their immediate successors, which is in nothing more marked than just in the slight grasp which the latter have on the principles of evangelical religion."[65] In the same year James Orr, in his Elliot Lectures delivered before the Western Theological Seminary at Allegheny, Pennsylvania, which were published under the title *Progress of Dogma*, affirmed:

There is no question ..., from the Protestant, and I believe also from the Scriptural standpoint, but that the Church, from a very early period, went seriously astray in its doctrinal and practical apprehension of the divine method of the sinner's salvation. Many beautiful utterances, I know, can be cited to show that the thought of acceptance through God's grace, on the grounds of Christ's merit alone, was never absent from the consciousness of the Church – nay, was its deepest note all through. But these cannot overbear the fact that ideas early crept in, and came to have controlling influence, which were in principle antagonistic to that consciousness. Partly, no doubt, this was due to the inevitable blunting of Pauline ideas in their passing over to the Gentile world, imperfectly prepared, through lack of a training under the

---

[64] Kenneth Escott Kirk, *The Vision of God: The Christian Doctrine of the Summum Bonum* (1928 Bampton Lectures; London: Longmans, Green, 1931), 111.

[65] Benjamin B. Warfield, "The Significance of the Westminster Standards as a Creed," *Selected Shorter Writings of Benjamin B. Warfield*, edited by John E. Meeter (Nutley, N. J.: Presbyterian and Reformed, 1970), 2.660.

law, to receive them; partly, also, is attributable to the fact already noticed, that, in order of time, the doctrines of sin, grace and atonement, which are the presuppositions of this doctrine of justification, had not yet been theologically investigated. But the main source of error must unquestionably be sought in the early introduction into the Church of, and the place given to, the *sacramentarian* principle, which, wherever it enters, is bound to exercise a disturbing influence on doctrine.... First came the connection of regeneration and forgiveness of sins with baptism—the doctrine of *baptismal regeneration*. In train of this, as its natural consequence, came the use of the term "justification"...to mean, not, as in Pauline usage, the *absolving* of a sinner from guilt, and *declaring* him to be righteous in God's sight, on the ground of what Christ has done for him, but peculiarly the *making* of the sinner righteous by the infusing into him a new nature, then on the ground of this *justitia infusia* declaring him righteous. We have next the still more serious restriction of this benefit to the cleansing away of sins committed *before* baptism, so that post-baptismal sins, as not covered by the initial justification, had to be expiated in some other way, by good works and satisfactions of the sinner's own. On the ground thus laid was built in due course the whole elaborate system of penance in the Romish Church...—its scheme of satis-factions, of purgatorial suffering for sins not completely satisfied for on earth, of masses and indulgences as a means of relief from these pains of the life beyond.[66]

About the Apostolic Fathers' understanding in the first three centuries concerning the work of Christ and concerning

---

[66] James Orr, *Progress of Dogma*, (Old Tappan, N.J.: Revell, n.d.), 247-49.

faith and good works Louis Berkhof, professor of systematic theology at Calvin Seminary from 1906 to 1944, writes:

> The work of Christ as the Redeemer [is] sometimes...seen in the fact that He...revealed the Father and taught the moral law. In some cases the death of Christ is represented...as opening the way for a new obedience, rather than as the ground of man's justification. This moralistic strain is, perhaps, the weakest point in the teachings of the Apostolic Fathers.
>
> ...Man is said to be justified by faith, but...an anti-Pauline strain of legalism becomes manifest at this point. Faith is simply the first step in the way of life, on which the moral development of the individual depends. But after the forgiveness of sins is once granted in baptism and apprehended by faith, man next merits this blessing by his good works, which become a second and independent principle alongside of faith. Christianity is often represented as a *nova lex*, and love, leading on to a new obedience, takes the leading place.
>
> ...in spite of all their emphasis on the grace of God and on faith as the appropriating organ of salvation, the early fathers [of the first three centuries] reveal a moralism that is not in harmony with the Pauline doctrine of salvation....
>
> [They place repentance alongside faith, and the external penitential] deeds [of repentance] are...regarded as having expiatory value in atoning for sins committed after baptism. There is a tendency to stress the necessity of good works,...to attach special merit to these, and to co-ordinate them with faith as a means of securing the divine favor. The view taken of good works is legal rather than evangelical. This moralistic perversion of New Testament Christianity found its explanation in the natural self-

righteousness of the human heart, and opened a doorway through which a Judaistic legalism entered the church.

...The idea is widely prevalent among them that baptism carries with it the forgiveness of previous sins, and that pardon for sins committed after baptism can be obtained by penance. Moreover, the thought...gradually [gained] ground that the good works of some, and especially the sufferings of the martyrs, may serve to atone for the sins of others. Toward the end of this period an excessive value is ascribed to the intercessions of confessors and martyrs, though some of the Church Fathers discourage this idea. [Citing Sohm, Berkhof] finds the explanation for this departure from the teachings of Scripture in the fact that "the natural man is a born Catholic."[67]

In his *A History of Christian Doctrine* J. L. Neve, professor in Hamma Divinity School, Wittenberg College, Springfield, Ohio, reaches similar conclusions,[68] as does J. N. D. Kelly, principal of St. Edmund Hall, Oxford, in his *Early Christian Doctrines.*[69] Richard Lovelace, professor of church history at Gordon-Conwell Divinity School, affirms: "By the early second century it is clear that Christians had come to think of themselves *as being justified through being sanctified,* accepted as righteous according to their actual obedience to the new Law of Christ."[70] And Thomas F. Torrance, professor of Christian

---

[67] Louis Berkhof, *The History of Christian Doctrines* (Edinburgh: Banner of Truth, 1975 reprint of 1937 edition), 40-1, 204-5.

[68] J. L. Neve, *A History of Christian Thought* (Philadelphia: Muhlenberg, 1946), I. 37-9.

[69] J. N. D. Kelly, *Early Christian Doctrine* (London: Adam & Charles Black, 1958), 163-4, 165, 168-9, 177-8, 184.

[70] Richard Lovelace, "A Call to Historic Roots and Continuity" in *The Orthodox Evangelicals,* edited by Robert Webber and Donald Bloesch (Nashville, Thomas Nelson, 1978), 49, emphasis supplied.

dogmatics at New College, Edinburgh from 1952 to 1979, in his *The Doctrine of Grace in the Apostolic Fathers*— whose entire work enquires into the literature of the Apostolic Fathers, that is to say, into the Didache of the Twelve Apostles, the First Epistle of Clement, the Epistles of Ignatius, the Epistle of Polycarp, the Epistle of Barnabas, the Shepherd of Hermas, and the Second Epistle of Clement, in order to discern how and why such a great divergence away from the teaching of the New Testament occurred in their understanding of salvation—concludes his doctoral research by saying:

In the Apostolic Fathers grace did not have [the] radical character [that it had in the New Testament]. The great presupposition of the Christian life, for them, was not a deed of decisive significance that cut across human life and set it on a wholly new basis grounded upon the self-giving of God. What took absolute precedence was God's call to a new life in obedience to revealed truth. Grace, as far as it was grasped, was subsidiary to that. And so religion was thought of primarily in terms of man's acts toward God, *in the striving toward justification*, much less in terms of God's acts for man which put him in the right with God once and for all.

...Salvation is wrought, they thought, certainly by divine pardon but on the ground of repentance, not apparently on the ground of the death of Christ alone...It was not seen that the whole of salvation is centred in the person and death of Christ, for there God has Himself come into the world and wrought a final act of redemption which undercuts all our own endeavours at self-justification, and places us in an entirely new situation in which faith alone saves a man, and through which alone is a man free to do righteousness spontaneously under the constraining love of Christ. That was not understood by the Apostolic

Fathers, and it is the primary reason for the degeneration of their Christian faith into something so different from the New Testament.[71]

C. N. Moody in his *The Mind of the Early Converts* declares that while

there was a conscious attempt by Ignatius and Polycarp ...to imitate Paul...it is obvious that they did not understand him. His "in Christ" theology, or Christ mysticism as it has been called, is not to be found in the second century; faith becomes mere belief, grace a commodity, justification a mere formula even on the lips of his most zealous imitators.

After looking with some care at the leading writers of this period, Moody concludes

---

[71] Thomas F. Torrance, *The Doctrine of Grace in the Apostolic Fathers* (Grand Rapids: Eerdmans, 1959), 133, 138, emphasis supplied. I cite Torrance at some length on this matter only because my own research bears out his conclusion, but I would not want to be perceived as endorsing another conviction of his, namely, that Westminster Calvinism is a betrayal of Calvin's theology in that it affirms (1) a double predestination, (2) a limited atonement, and (3) an incarnational redemption (see his *Scottish Theology from John Knox to John McLeod Campbell* [Edinburgh: T. & T. Clark, 1996]).

J. I. Packer, in his "What Did the Cross Achieve?; The Logic of Penal Substitution," *Collected Shorter Writings of J. I Packer* (Carlisle, Cumbria, UK: Paternoster, 1998), 91, fn. 7, thinks that the thesis of Torrance which I endorse is "sharp-edged" and needs the qualification that the patristic period's experience of redemption was far richer than its attempted formulations of this experience. In my judgment Packer's observation is wishful thinking; Torrance's thesis is borne out by the patristic literature itself and his point is enunciated by many scholars writing both before and after him.

[1] that the majority of the Christians had about as much theology in them as the Epistle of James;...[2] that the giants of New Testament theology, Paul and John, were simply not understood; and [3] that the great doctrines they taught were hardly ever assimilated. Grace, justification, sanctification, union with Christ and the other great evangelical doctrines that meant so much to the apostles Paul, John, Peter and the writer to the Hebrews, had been largely jettisoned and replaced with a new legalism in ethics and a Christology which lost interest in the humanity of Jesus.[72]

Basing his objection largely on statements from the anonymous *Epistle to Diognetus*, Michael Green believes that this "Harnack to Torrance view" is "gravely exaggerated,"[73] yet he admits that Ignatius and Hermas made too much of the sacraments, the latter even equating the gospel with the law of God, and finally even he has to conclude:

Very soon the Church became obsessed with subjects like what was to be done with post-baptismal sin, and it was a short step from there to reparation, atoning for past misdeeds and the like, which came to its full flower in the Church of the Middle Ages....The future is seen entirely in terms of rewards for the virtuous and punishments for the damned...The subapostolic age thought, no doubt, that they were teaching New Testament Christianity: in fact they lived in another realm altogether.[74]

---

[72] Cited by Michael Green, *Evangelism in the Early Church* (Guildford: Eagle, 1995 reprint of 1970 edition), 160. I inserted the bracketed numbers to aid the reader—RLR.

[73] Green, *Evangelism in the Early Church*, 166.

[74] Green, *Evangelism in the Early Church*, 168, 169.

In light of what he finally concludes about the pronouncements of these Fathers of early Christianity, it is difficult, to say no more, to see why Green would say that this "Harnack to Torrance view"—shared by liberal and orthodox alike—is "gravely exaggerated."

Whatever one finally concludes about details, it appears to be incontrovertibly clear, as I have already indicated,[75] that the post-apostolic church's sub-Pauline soteriological deliverances launched the church on a doctrinal trajectory

---

[75] As I already stated, there was always an elect "remnant" by grace who believed the true gospel. Two impressive illustrations of this remnant are Anselm and John Staupitz. Anselm, Archbishop of Canterbury (1033-1109), wrote a tract to console the dying who were alarmed on account of their sin (see his *Opera*, Migne, 1:686-7), from which the following is extracted:

Question: Do you believe that the Lord Jesus died for you? Answer: I believe it.

Question: Do you thank him for his passion and death? Answer: I do thank him.

Question: Do you believe that you cannot be saved except by his death? Answer: I believe it.

Anselm then addresses the dying man: "Come then, while life remains in you, *in his death alone place your whole trust; in nothing else place any trust*; to his death commit yourself wholly; *with this alone cover yourself wholly*; and if the Lord your God wills to judge you, say: 'Lord, between your judgment and me I present the death of our Lord Jesus Christ; in no other way can I contend with you.' And if he shall say that you are a sinner, say: 'Lord, I interpose the death of our Lord Jesus Christ between my sins and you.' If he should say that you deserve condemnation, say: 'Lord, I set the death of our Lord Jesus Christ between my evil deserts and you, and his merits I offer for those which I ought to have and have not.' If he says that he is angry with you, say: 'Lord, I oppose the death of our Lord Jesus Christ between your wrath and me.' And when you have completed this, say again: 'Lord, I set the death of our Lord Jesus Christ between me and you.'"

in the area of soteriology that moved virtually the entire church away from the pristine Pauline teaching on salvation by pure grace and justification by faith alone, a trajectory that eventually came to expression in Semi-Pelagianism and Semi-Semi-Pelagianism, that found popular expression in the slogan of late medieval scholasticism, "God will not deny his grace to those who do what lies within their power,"[76]

John Staupitz (d. 1524), the vicar-general of the Augustinian Order for all Germany, one day asked the young Martin Luther: "*Why* are you so sad, brother Martin?" "Ah," replied the young Luther, "I do not know what will become of me…It is in vain that I make promises to God; sin is ever the stronger." To this Staupitz replied:

O my friend, more than a thousand times have I sworn to our holy God to live piously, and I have never kept my vows. Now I swear no longer, for I know that I cannot keep my solemn promises. If God will not be merciful towards me for the love of Christ, and grant me a happy departure when I must quit this world, *I shall never, with the aid of all my vows and all my good works, stand before him*. I must perish.

Why do you torment yourself…? Look at the wounds of Jesus Christ, to the blood that he has shed for you; it is there that the grace of God will appear to you. Instead of torturing yourself on account of your sins, throw yourself into the Redeemer's arms. Trust in him—in the righteousness of his life—in the atonement of his death. Do not shrink back…Listen to the Son of God. He became man to give you the assurance of divine favor." Cited by J. H. Merle D'Aubigne, *The Life and Times of Martin Luther* (Reprint; Chicago: Moody, 1978) 37-8.

There were also the Waldenses who followed the teaching of Peter Waldo, the Lollards who followed the teaching of John Wycliffe, and the Bohemians who followed the teaching of John Hus. Such examples give us reason to believe that the New Testament doctrine of justification by faith alone was implicitly, if not explicitly, held by many other pious souls throughout all the ages of papal darkness.

[76] This theological heresy is popularly expressed today by the oft-heard assertion: "God helps those who help themselves."

and formal expression in the sacerdotal system of Thomas
Aquinas, which in turn finally became the hardened official
position of the Roman Catholic Church at the Council of
Trent and which continues to be the official position of the
Roman communion to the present day. Bear with me as I
elaborate now upon these observations.

The Church's Drift into Soteriological Apostasy

This *naturalistic* soteriological vision (for that is what it
is) in its *purest* expression, which Benjamin B. Warfield
designated "autosoterism" ("self-salvation"), the church has
called "Pelagianism" named for Pelagius, the late-fourth/
early-fifth-century British monk who formally taught it. This
vision contends that men can save themselves, that is to say,
that *their native powers are such that men are capable of
doing everything that God requires of them for salvation.*
     Over against this soteric plan, the *supernaturalistic*
vision, designated "Augustinianism" after Augustine (354-
430), bishop of Hippo, who vigorously resisted Pelagius'
teachings with his own teachings on sin and grace, insists
that *men are incapable of saving themselves and that all
the powers essential to the saving of the soul must come
from a gracious God.* Augustinianism triumphed formally,
if not actually, over Pelagianism in A.D. 418 when
Pelagianism was condemned at the Sixteenth Council of
Carthage. In this conciliar triumph, Warfield notes: "...it
was once for all settled that Christianity was to remain a
religion, and a religion for sinful men, and not rot down into
a mere ethical system, fitted only for the righteous who need
no salvation."[77] In other words, the church of Jesus Christ,
alone among all the religions of the world in this regard, in

---

[77] Benjamin B. Warfield, *The Plan of Salvation* (reprint; Grand Rapids:
Eerdmans, n.d.), 36.

its best creedal moments is "supernaturalistic" or "Augustinian" in its soteric conception that God must save man, and every Christian *should be* in this sense "Augustinian" in his soteric beliefs.[78]

But as I just intimated, Pelagianism did not die with its conciliar condemnation in A.D. 418, men and women being born as they are with Pelagian hearts which fact makes it necessary to fight this battle in every generation. Rather, it

---

[78] I do not mean to suggest by what I just said that Augustine always held consistently to this supernaturalistic principle, for it is a matter of simple historical record that he did not. In Augustine one can find the doctrine both of salvation by grace through faith and the blurring of that vision by a salvation dispensed through the church and its sacraments (see L. Berkhof, *Systematic Theology*, 559). The former may be found expressed, for example, in his *Confessions* when he writes: "You converted me to yourself so that I no longer sought…any of this world's promises" (8:12), and again, *"By your gift* I had come totally not to will what I had willed but to will what you willed" (9.1, emphasis supplied). Clearly, Augustine understood that his conversion was entirely the work of God's grace. But the latter may also be found in his *Confessions* when he writes: "I recognized the act of your will, and I gave praise to your name, rejoicing in faith. But this faith would not let me feel safe about my past sins, since your baptism had not yet come to remit them" (9.4). Augustine then declares that, after Ambrose baptized him, "all anxiety as to our past life fled away" (9.6). And as for justification, interpreting as he did the Latin verb *iustificare* ("to justify") as *iustum facere* ("to make righteous"), Augustine understood justifying righteousness as an *internal* righteousness, something that God works *within* us. Warfield seems quite justified, then, in observing that the Protestant Reformation, especially on the Reformed side, was the revolt of Augustine's doctrine of grace against his doctrine of the church, a revolt against seeing grace channeled through the sacraments, a revolt, in all Reformational expressions, against the notion that predestination trickled only through the narrow crevices of church ordinances. The Reformation was, by contrast, an affirmation of Augustine's grasp upon human lostness, bondage to what is dark and wrong, the indispensability of grace, and the glory of the gospel because of him in whom the good news took and takes form.

only went underground, "meanwhile vexing the Church with modified forms of itself, modified just enough to escape the letter of the Church's condemnation."[79] For example, it reappeared at once in the Semi-Pelagian denial of the necessity of *prevenient* grace for salvation. This Semi-Pelagianism was opposed by the Second Council of Orange —not an ecumenical council—in A.D. 529.

Alister E. McGrath, lecturer in historical and systematic theology at Wycliffe Hall, Oxford since 1983, after noting correctly in his study, *Luther's Theology of the Cross*, that the earlier pronouncements of the Sixteenth Council of Carthage were "vague at several points which were to prove of significance, and these were revised at what is generally regarded as being the most important council of the early church to deal with the doctrine of justification—the Second Council of Orange, convened in 529,"[80] then observes:

No other council was convened to discuss the doctrine of justification between [529] and 1545, when the Council of Trent assembled to debate that doctrine, among many other things. There was thus a period of over a millennium during which the teaching office of the church remained silent on the issue of justification. This silence serves to further enhance the importance of the pronouncements of Orange II on the matter, as these thus come to represent the definitive teaching of the Christian church on the doctrine of justification during the medieval period, before the Council of Trent was convened. Recent scholarship has established that no theologian of the Middle Ages ever cites the decisions of Orange II, or shows the slightest awareness of the existence of such

---

[79] Warfield, *The Plan of Salvation*, 36.
[80] Alister E. McGrath, *Luther's Theology of the Cross* (Oxford: Blackwell, 1985), 11.

decisions. For reasons which we simply do not understand, from the tenth century until the assembly of the Council of Trent in 1545, the theologians of the western church appear to be unaware of the existence of such a council, let alone its pronouncements. The theologians of the Middle Ages were thus obliged to base their teaching on justification on the canons of the Council of Carthage, which were simply incapable of bearing the strain which came to be placed upon them. The increasing precision of the technical terms employed within the theological schools inevitably led to the somewhat loose terms used by the Council of Carthage being interpreted in a manner quite alien to that intended by those who originally employed them.[81]

But in spite of the generally-ignored good work of the Second Council of Orange against Semi-Pelagianism's denial of the necessity of *prevenient* grace for salvation, regrettably that same council, by not decisively accepting Augustine's doctrines of sin and predestination, betrayed the church into the Semi-Semi-Pelagian denial of the *irresistibility* of that prevenient grace by human free will. The certain efficacy of saving grace, that is, its irresistibility, was ignored by the Council of Orange, and "thus," writes Benjamin Warfield,

> the conquering march of Augustinianism was checked and the pure confession of salvation by grace alone made forever impossible within that section of the Church whose proud boast is that it is *semper eadem* ["always the same"]. It was no longer legally possible...to ascribe salvation so entirely to the grace of God that it could complete itself without the aid of the discredited human

---

[81] McGrath, *Luther's Theology of the Cross*, 11-12.

will—its aid only as empowered and moved by prevenient grace indeed, but not effectually moved, so that it could not hold back and defeat the operations of saving grace.[82]

This theological vision eventually came to expression in the popular slogan of the late medieval Schoolmen: "God will not deny his grace to those who do what lies within their power" (see William of Occam's *facere quod in se est*, "doing what in you is").[83] So in spite of recurring protests through the centuries by some theologians (for example, Gottschalk in the ninth century, Bradwardine in the fourteenth), eventually Thomas Aquinas, as we have already noted, systematized this theological vision[84] and the Council of

---

[82] Warfield, *The Plan of Salvation*, 37.

[83] Martin Luther remarked: "[The] arguments of the Scholastics about the merit of congruence and of worthiness (*de merito congrui et condigni*) are nothing but vain figments and dreamy speculations of idle folk about worthless stuff. Yet they form the foundation of the papacy, and on them it rests to this very day. For this is what every monk imagines: By observing the sacred duties of my order I can earn the grace of congruence, but by the works I do after I have received this grace I can accumulate a merit so great that it will not only be enough to bring me to eternal life but enough to sell and give it to others." He says further: "There is no such thing as merit; but all who are justified are justified for nothing (*gratis*), and this is credited to no one but to the grace of God." Still further he states: "For Christ alone it is proper to help and save others with His merits and works. The works of others are of benefit to no one, not to themselves either; for the statement stands: 'The just shall live by faith' (Rom. 1:17)." (*What Luther Says: An Anthology* [Saint Louis: Concordia, 1959], 2, 921-2.

[84] In his article, "Aquinas Was a Protestant," which appeared in the May 1994 issue of *Tabletalk*, the popular monthly devotional publication of Ligonier Ministries, Inc., edited by R. C. Sproul, Jr., John H. Gerstner declares that Aquinas "was a medieval Protestant teaching the Reformation doctrine of justification by faith alone" (13)—indeed, who "taught the biblical doctrine of justification" (14)—and "one of Protestantism's greatest theologians" (14). While he acknowledges that

Trent (1545) declared it to be the official position of those churches in communion with Counter-Reformation Rome.[85] While it is true that the Second Council of Orange (A.D.

Augustine did not adequately develop the forensic element in justification, he asserts that Aquinas "was not led astray" but "with Augustine taught the biblical doctrine of justification so that if the Roman church had followed Aquinas the Reformation would not have been absolutely necessary" (14). He calls the supposition, drawn by both Roman Catholic and Protestant theologians alike, that Aquinas was a "modern tridentine Romanist" a "pernicious error" (14). He draws these conclusions because, he says, "Aquinas taught a doctrine of *iustificatio impii*, a justification of the impious" (14).

In my opinion Gerstner's contention, to say the least, is grossly in error. He is asking us to believe that for seven hundred years now no one except the Council of Trent "read" Aquinas correctly (and that Council, he avers, was "horrified" at what it read and rejected his view on justification), and that it is now he, without benefit of the discovery of a lost manuscript by Aquinas which throws new light on his intentions in his *Summa*, who is again reading Aquinas aright. Stranger things have happened in church history, I suppose, but I cannot think of one offhand. One may be pardoned were he to conclude that it is far more likely that it is Dr. Gerstner who is misreading Aquinas. Furthermore, the "pernicious errorists" to whom he refers above would have to include the two great reformers Martin Luther and John Calvin, for neither of them claimed Aquinas for the Reformation cause. Indeed, Luther, with characteristic bombast, spoke of him as "the *fountain* [*Brunn*] and *original soup* [*Grundsuppe*] of *all heresy, error, and Gospel havoc* [*aller Ketzerei, Irrthumb und Vertilgung des Evangelium*], as his books bear witness" (Schaff, *History*, V, 676). And Calvin declared that the definition of justification which the Council of Trent proffered at length "contains nothing else than the trite dogma of the schools [of which Aquinas was the most mature representative—RLR]: that men are justified partly by the grace of God and partly by their own works" ("On the Sixth Session of the Council of Trent," *Acts of the Council of Trent with the Antidote* [Grand Rapids: Baker, 1983 reprint of Calvin's *Tracts*], 3, 108). David S. Schaff's representative remarks, found in Philip Schaff's *History of the Christian Church* (Grand Rapids: Eerdmans, 1960 reproduction of the 1907 edition), V, 662, 675, 754, 756, clearly are on the mark:

529) did not accept and profess Augustine's doctrine of predestination—indeed, the council was *almost* completely silent about election and *was* completely silent about the *irresistibility* of grace—the council's scripture citations were so appropriate in its opposition to early sixth-century semi-Pelagianism that the same texts appeared again and again in the preaching and writings of the sixteenth-century Reformers, creating for the Council of Trent the necessity of having to use Orange's texts without lapsing into the Reformers' *sola fide*. Trent believed that it did this, namely, that it walked the tightrope between Pelagianism and Semi-Pelagianism on the one hand and the Reformers' doctrine

---

In the teachings of Thomas Aquinas we have, with one or two exceptions [the Protestant doctrine of justification not being one of them—RLR] the doctrinal tenets of the Latin Church in their perfect exposition as we have them in the Decrees of the council of Trent in their final statement...the theology of the Angelic doctor and the theology of the Roman Catholic Church are identical in all particulars except the immaculate conception. He who understands Thomas understands the mediaeval theology at its best a .; will be in possession of the doctrinal system of the Roman Church...No distinction was made by the mediaeval theologians between the doctrine of *justification* and the doctrine of *sanctification*, such as is made by Protestant theologians. Justification was treated as a process of making the sinner righteous, and not as a judicial sentence by which he was declared to be righteous...Although several of Paul's statements in the Epistle to the Romans are quoted by Thomas Aquinas, neither he nor the other Schoolmen rise to the idea that it is upon the [condition] of faith that a man is justified. Faith is a virtue, not a justifying principle, and is treated at the side of hope and love.

For my complete response see my article, "Dr. John H. Gerstner on Thomas Aquinas as a Protestant," *Westminster Theological Journal* 59, no. 1 (1997): 113-21.

[85] Regrettably, this same denial of the irresistibility of divine grace by the power of the human will was later espoused by Jacobus Arminius and his followers, whose numbers are legion today.

of grace on the other when it rejected Augustine's and the Reformers' doctrine of human depravity and asserted that the freedom of man's will, *though weakened by sin*, may still choose between incompatible courses of action and may be fully recovered through a divine act in baptism. But in doing so, even though Rome's own great humanist scholar Desiderius Erasmus of Rotterdam and other of Rome's brightest philologists had by this time uncovered the fact that Jerome's Latin Vulgate had mistranslated the Greek verb μετανοέω (*metanoeō*, "repent") as "do penance" and the Greek verb δικαιόω (*dikaioō*, "*declare* righteous") as "*make* righteous," the Council of Trent, by insisting as it did upon the necessity of man's cooperation with grace in salvation, rejected the Pauline doctrine of justification by pure grace alone through faith alone and substituted for it Rome's doctrine of justification by faith and works.[86]

Modern Attempts of *Rapprochement*

Regrettably, Roman Catholic error continues unabated into our day with less and less opposition from a much-divided and theologically illiterate Protestantism. In fact, in very recent times there has even been a mad rush on the part of some heirs of the Reformation to establish a *rapprochement* with Rome as evidenced here in North America by the two recent, shall I say, concordats, "Evangelicals and Catholics Together: The Christian Mission in the Third Millennium" and "The Gift of Salvation," both of which are capitulations to the Roman Catholic view of justification, and on the European continent by the document, "The Joint Declaration on the Doctrine of Justification."

---

[86] For a contemporary argument for Rome's position on justification, see the Appendix on Robert A. Sungenis' *"Not By Faith Alone: The Biblical Evidence for the Catholic Doctrine of Justification.*

"Evangelicals and Catholics Together"

The first of the North American documents, "Evangelicals
and Catholics Together," which appeared in *First Things*
(May 1994), is a statement composed by eight Protestants
(led by Charles Colson) and seven Roman Catholics (led by
Fr. Richard John Neuhaus, Director of the Institute on
Religion and Public Life) and endorsed by twelve other
Protestants and thirteen other Roman Catholics. While its
call for co-belligerence against the rampant moral
degeneracy in our nation's political, legal, medical,
educational, and cultural life and for cooperation against
social injustice and economic poverty is appropriate enough
(Section IV), the statement's marginalizing of many of the
stark theological differences which exist between
Protestantism and Roman Catholicism is inexcusable when
its authors affirm their agreement on the Apostles' Creed
and on the proposition that "we are justified by grace through
faith because of Christ" (Section I) and then on this
"confessional" basis call for an end to proselytizing each
other's communicants and for a missiological ecumenism
which cooperates together in evangelism and spiritual nurture
(Section V).[87] The word "alone" after the word "faith" in the
statement's proposition on justification is thundering by its

---

[87] I am disappointed that Dr. James I. Packer, one of the statement's
Protestant endorsers, lends the enormous prestige of his name and his
leadership position among evangelicals to this ecumenical statement,
even though he affirms in his "apology" entitled, "Why I Signed It"
(*Christianity Today* [Dec 12, 1994], 34-7), (1) that Rome's claim to be
the only institution that can without qualification be called the church of
Christ is theologically and historically flawed; (2) that Rome's teaching
on the Mass and on merit cuts across Paul's doctrine of justification in
and through Christ by faith; (3) that all of Rome's forms of the Mary
cult, its invoking of saints, its belief in purgatory, and its continuing
disbursement of indulgences, to say the least, "damp down the full

absence. As written, the statement is a capitulation to Rome's understanding of the doctrine, for never in the debate between Rome and the first Protestant reformers did anyone on either side deny that sinners must be justified by faith. The whole controversy in the sixteenth century turned on whether sinners were justified by *faith alone* (*sola fide*) or by faith *and* good works which earn merit before God. The Protestant reformers, following Paul's teaching on justification in Galatians and Romans, affirmed the former and denied the latter; Rome denied the former and affirmed the latter. And the Protestant reformers, again following Paul (compare his entire argument in Galatians), maintained that the path the sinner follows here leads either to heaven or to hell. The Reformers of the sixteenth century—over against Rome's doctrine of salvation which was and still is essential to the maintenance of its priestcraft and thus its economic fortunes—being the biblical scholars that they were, rejected Rome's soteriology with all of its concomitant errors and returned to the earlier best insights of the later Augustine and before him—and more importantly—to the inspired insights, in particular, of Paul's letters to the Galatians and to the Romans. Through their careful study of Scripture they came to understand that

1. the only way to have and to retain the *solus Christus*[88] ("Christ alone") of salvation is to insist upon the *sola fide* ("faith alone") of justification;

---

assurance to which, according to Scripture, justification should lead through the ministry of the Holy Spirit"; and (4) that Rome's claim of infallibility for all conciliar and some papal pronouncements and its insistence that Christians should take their beliefs from the church rather than from the Bible make self-correction virtually impossible.

[88] Protestants do not believe in *solus Christus* in an all-exclusive sense because Paul expressly teaches that we must believe also in the Father

2. the Christian's righteousness before God is *in heaven* at the right hand of God in Jesus Christ, and *not on earth* within the believer;

3. saving faith is to be directed to the doing and dying of Christ alone and to no degree to the good works or inner experience of the believer;

4. the ground of our justification is the vicarious work of Christ *for* us, not the gracious work of the Spirit *in* us;

5. the only man with whom the infinitely holy God can have *direct* fellowship is the perfect Godman and only mediator "between God and men, the man Christ Jesus" (1 Tim 2:5), and that it is only as sinful people place their trust in Christ's saving work and are thereby regarded by God as "in Christ" (the apostle Paul's great ἐν Χριστῷ [*en Christō*] formula) that the triune God can have any fellowship with them;

(and by extension in the Spirit) if we would be justified (Rom 4:5, 23). But it is true that we trust in Christ's preceptive and penal obedience alone for our justification. Indeed, that is why we are Protestants: we take seriously not only the "big" words of Scripture, such as "predestination," "justification," and "sanctification," but the "little" words as well, specifically, the little word "one" (εἷς, *heis*), which is virtually the *solus* in *solus Christus*, and which by implication carries along with it the *sola's* of *sola gratia* and *sola fide*) in the Pauline phrases: "the *one* man Jesus Christ" (Rom 5:15), "through the *one*, Jesus Christ" (Rom 5:17), "through *one* act of righteousness" (Rom 5:18), "through the obedience of the *one*" (Rom 5:19), and "there is...*one* mediator between God and men, the man Christ Jesus" (1 Tim 2:5). We add to the obedient work of this *one* man *nothing*—not our "works of righteousness" which are as menstrual rags (Tit 3:5; see Isa 64:6), not the supposed works of supererogation of Mary, not the supposed works of supererogation of Catholicism's designated saints, *not anything!* "*Jesus* paid it all; all to *him* I owe. Sin had left a crimson stain; *he* washed it white as snow."

6. the faith-righteousness of justification is not personal but vicarious, not infused but imputed, not experiential but judicial, not psychological but legal, not our own but a righteousness alien to us, and not earned but graciously given (*sola gratia*) through faith in Christ which is itself a gift of grace; all of which mean

7. that justification by faith is not to be set off in our thinking over against justification by works as such but over against justification by *our* works, for justification is indeed grounded in Christ's alien active and passive work in our stead which we receive by faith alone.

For them these tenets meant practically and existentially, as Martin Luther writes, that

a Christian is at once a sinner and a saint; he is wicked and pious at the same time. For so far as our persons are concerned, we are in sins and are sinners in our own name. But Christ brings us another name, in which there is the forgiveness of sins, that for His sake sins are remitted and pardoned. So both statements are true: There are sins, for the old Adam is not entirely dead as yet; yet the sins are *not* there. The reason is this: For Christ's sake God does not want to see them. I have my eyes on them. I feel and see them well enough. But there is Christ, commanding that I be told that I should repent, that is, confess myself a sinner and believe the forgiveness of sins in His name. For repentance, remorse, and knowledge of sin, though necessary, is not enough; faith in the forgiveness of sins in the name of Jesus must be added. But where there is such faith, God no longer sees any sins; for then you stand before God, not in your name but in Christ's name. He adorns you with grace and righteousness, although in your own eyes and personally you are a poor sinner, full of weakness and unbelief.[89]

And it is the Protestant teaching on justification by faith alone, Luther contended in the *Schmalcald Articles* of 1537, that

> must be believed and cannot be obtained or apprehended by any work, law, or merit...nothing in this article [of faith] can be given up or compromised, even if heaven and earth and things temporal should be destroyed...On this article rests all that we teach and practice against the pope, the devil, and the world. Therefore we must be quite certain and have no doubts about it. Otherwise all is lost, and the pope, the devil, and all our adversaries will gain the victory.

"The Gift of Salvation"

The second North American document, "The Gift of Salvation," also appeared in *First Things* (January 1998). After affirming at some length some very fine things about the doctrine of justification, concerning which the framers of the document declare: "We understand that what we here affirm is in agreement with what the Reformation traditions have meant by justification by faith alone (*sola fide*)," it immediately continues with the remark: "In justification we receive the gift of the Holy Spirit, through whom the love of God is poured forth into our hearts (Romans 5:5)." Now if they had written: "In regeneration we receive the gift of the Holy Spirit..." we would take no umbrage; if they had written: "In *conjunction with* justification we receive the gift of the Holy Spirit..." we would not quibble. But when

---

[89] Martin Luther, *What Luther Says: An Anthology*, edited by Ewald M. Plass (St. Louis, Missouri: Concordia, 1959), 1, 522.

the framers state: "*In justification* we receive the gift of the Holy Spirit..." they fall into the Roman Catholic error of confusing justification and sanctification and thereby endorse the Roman Catholic view of justification. Then in their conclusion the framers of the document "rejoice in the unity we have discovered and are confident of the fundamental truths about the gift of salvation we have affirmed," but they immediately acknowledge that "there are necessarily interrelated questions that require further and urgent exploration" such as

> the meaning of baptismal regeneration, the Eucharist, and sacramental grace; the historic uses of the language of justification as it relates to imputed and transformative righteousness; the normative status of justification in relation to all other Christian doctrine; the assertion that while justification is by faith alone, the faith that receives salvation is never alone; diverse understandings of merit, reward, purgatory, and indulgences; Marian devotion and the assistance of the saints in the life of salvation; and the possibility of salvation for those who have not been evangelized.

But how these signatories believe they have come to agreement upon justification when they have not addressed some of the most glaring areas of discord between Roman Catholicism and Protestantism, all of which overthrow the Protestant doctrine of justification, is, for me, a mystery! Surely D. A. Carson, professor of New Testament at Trinity Evangelical Divinity School, is right when he asserts that for most (I wish he could have said "all") evangelicals,

> our understanding of justification is tied to a rejection of purgatory, indulgences, and claims that Mary may properly

be called a coredemptrix. For us the doctrine of purgatory (to go no further) implicitly asserts that the death of Christ on the cross for sinners was in itself insufficient or inadequate. Catholics, within a quite different framework, draw no such conclusion. Sooner or later, of course, the dispute over purgatory gets tracked farther back to the dispute over the locus of revelation. It is very difficult [I would say impossible—RLR] to substantiate purgatory from the Protestant Bible. Catholics themselves commonly appeal to the Apocrypha (especially 2 Macc 12:46) and tradition.[90] Suddenly our reflections on justification become inextricably intertwined with complex debates not only over purgatory but also over Scripture and tradition, papal authority, and so forth. This is not an attempt to blow smoke over an already confusing terrain. It is simply a way of saying that...to formulate a shared statement on justification without recognizing that the two sides bring diametrically opposed sets of baggage to the table, with the baggage intact when we walk away from the table, is to construct a chimera.[91]

"Joint Declaration on the Doctrine of Justification"

A brief discussion of the European "Joint Declaration on the Doctrine of Justification" is also necessary inasmuch as it is this document that is being widely hailed as having brought an end to the division created within Western

---

[90] Even here it is worth observing that the notion of purgatory receives no prominence in the Western church until the twelfth and thirteenth centuries, which with respect to a doctrine drawn primarily from tradition makes the doctrine of purgatory seem like a remarkably loose use of the Vincentian canon that the church should believe only those doctrines that have been believed by everyone everywhere and at all times.

[91] D. A. Carson, "Reflections on Salvation and Justification in the New Testament," *JETS* 40/4 (December 1997), 604.

Christendom by the Protestant Reformation of the sixteenth century. After many years of discussion the document was finalized in 1997 and submitted for adoption to the Magisterium of the Roman Catholic Church and to the member churches of the Lutheran World Federation (LWF). Eighty-one of the LWF's one hundred and twenty-four member denominations approved this eleven-page document by early 1998, and on June 16, 1998 the Council of the LWF approved it unanimously.[92] The generally positive official Roman Catholic response came nine days later, and on October 31, 1999 in Augsburg, Germany—the site of the drawing up of the Augsburg Confession and four hundred and eighty-two years to the day after Luther's posting of his Ninety-Five Theses—the Roman Catholic Church and the LWF signed the Official Common Statement (OCS) confirming the Joint Declaration.

---

[92] Thirty-five of the LWF's one hundred and twenty-four member churches did not vote on the Joint Declaration, five actually opposed it, and three of four responses which were difficult to interpret were judged by the LWF to be probably "no" votes. To these forty-three non-endorsing member churches may be added at least thirty other non-endorsing Lutheran church bodies in the world Lutheran community that are not member churches of the LWF. This means that of these one hundred and fifty-four Lutheran church bodies seventy-three of them (or slightly over forty-seven percent) have not endorsed the Joint Declaration. The LWF claims that it represents fifty-eight million of the world's sixty-two million Lutherans. But as a matter of fact the LWF has no authority to speak officially for a single one of its member churches. And since a significant percentage of the fifty-eight million Lutherans allegedly represented by the LWF comes from state churches that regard entire national populations as "Lutheran" even where the majority of persons never darken a church door, which is to say that the alleged number does not come from any direct measurement of actual church attendance, it is impossible to know how many truly evangelical Lutherans in actual fact the LWF signatories represented. I would guess the number to be relatively low.

Now what does this Joint Declaration accomplish? Does it articulate, as it claims, a "common understanding of justification" that "encompasses a consensus in the basic truths"? Not really. In fact, the Joint Declaration does not even *claim* to be a *synthesis* of two opposing doctrines of justification. Rather, it self-consciously represents itself as an exercise in "reconciled diversity," that is, a "differentiated consensus" of *two different doctrines* of justification. Having cast the Joint Declaration in the vague theological language that is characteristic of the work of the modern ecumenical movement, the subscribers of the Declaration, by their postmodern usage of theological terminology by which terms are used in such a way that both parties can read their respective positions into them, have not so much agreed with one another as they have reached a consensus on a minimal core of common Christian language and then agreed to condone a charitable rendering of one another's historic differences. Said another way, the document defines the consensus in terms of a "bidimensionality" in which it declares that on one level there is a fundamental commonality of the two doctrines of justification and on the other level there are remaining differences. This consensus claims that "the differing explications" of the doctrine of justification within their respective traditions are still "compatible" with the Joint Declaration; hence the occasion for some of Trent's doctrinal condemnations no longer exists provided certain conditions are present!

But let no one think that Rome has now adopted either Martin Luther's or historic Protestantism's understanding of justification. Not at all! The Vatican has made it quite clear that Trent's deliverances still stand as binding dogma for the Roman church. What the Vatican did by its signing the OCS confirming the Joint Declaration is simply to declare that Trent's condemnations of the Lutheran doctrine of justification are no longer valid *provided the OCS's statements about the Lutheran formulations "by faith alone" and* simul iustus et peccator *are interpreted in the Roman Catholic sense over against their Reformation meanings.* In other words, the Vatican is basically saying that even though it still believes the Lutheran view is in error in some very significant ways, it is now willing to view the Lutheran view as no longer a *church-dividing* doctrine. All the while it continues to articulate its own view of justification in its distinctly Tridentine manner.

What does the Joint Declaration say specifically is the "fundamental commonality" of the two traditions on justification? An orthodox Protestant can only gasp when he reads what the Joint Declaration hails in paragraph 15 as their "fundamental commonality":

Together we confess: By grace alone, in faith in Christ's saving work and not because of any merit on our part, we are accepted by God and receive the Holy Spirit, who renews our hearts while equipping and calling us to good works.[93]

This basic statement is then clarified in paragraphs 19, 22, 25, 28, 31, 34, and 37, allegedly developing the commonality on the basic truths of justification point by point, which commonality is essentially expressed simply by saying that God justifies by his love alone apart from human effort.

Both parties to the debate in the sixteenth century could

---

[93] The reader should compare the obfuscation of this definition of justification which confuses justification with sanctification with the clarity of the classic Protestant definition of justification in *Westminster Shorter Catechism*, Question 33: "Justification is an act of God's free grace, wherein he pardoneth all our sins, and accepteth us as righteous in his sight, only for the righteousness of Christ imputed to us, and received by faith alone."

have affirmed this phraseology under certain circumstances, but on the face of it, as a definition of justification it is inclined much more favorably toward Rome's teaching. For Trent never denied that justification comes by grace alone. Nor did Trent deny that justification is based entirely on Christ's saving work. Nor did Trent deny that God accepts us *initially* without regard to human merit. In fact, it affirmed these things. But Trent did deny that we receive this grace by faith alone, insisting that justifying faith must be clothed with love, with the Reformers countering that since love is the fulfillment of the law, Rome's representation, though veiled perhaps, is still a doctrine of justification by our works of congruent merit. And this congruent merit, Trent strongly maintained, plays a significant role in adding to God's grace, *thereby causing God ultimately to accept us as those who deserve his favor.* The magisterial reformers would have fiercely disavowed and opposed to the death this definition as a statement of *their* understanding of justification, for no mention is made of either Christ's work as the sole ground of justification or the imputation of Christ's righteousness to the sinner through faith apart from human works. Truth was of more consequence to them than any superficial show of church unity. Consequently, the Joint Declaration is in no way the "breakthrough" that it is being hailed as being concerning the doctrine that has divided Rome from Wittenberg. The adoption of the document by its signatories, given its faulty methodology, imprecise theological language, and ahistorical treatment of the foundational documents of Lutheranism, is simply the latest opportunity for Rome to appear ecumenical and the latest example of some Lutherans' willingness to sacrifice God's truth for the sake of a false church unity.

No document could illustrate more clearly than does this Joint Declaration that Rome has not abandoned its sub-

Pauline commitment to Trent's doctrine of justification by faith and works: Rome has not given up a thing by signing this Declaration. Rather, it was the liberal Lutheran signers, regrettably, who have been willing to compromise the great *solas* of the Reformation and the faith of their sixteenth-century "father" for the sake of a show of church unity with the church of Rome. Consequently, the Joint Declaration has done *nothing* to adjudicate the differences which arose at the time of the Reformation, for which many Protestants paid with their lives, but rather has simply interpreted those differences in a relatively mild way and then encourages, for the sake of Christian unity, the acceptance of each communion by the other. In sum, there is *no consensus* on the doctrine of justification in the Declaration but rather only an expressed willingness to overlook one another's "errors," presumably because church unity is to take precedence over doctrinal truth.

Anglican bishop J. C. Ryle's condemnation in his day of church unity without doctrinal unity applies, however, equally in our own day to such joint statements:

> We have no right to expect anything but the pure Gospel of Christ, unmixed and unadulterated,—the same Gospel that was taught by the Apostles,—to do good to the souls of men. I believe that to maintain this pure truth in the Church men should be ready to make any sacrifice, to hazard peace, to risk dissension, and run the risk of division. *They should no more tolerate false doctrine than they would tolerate sin.* They should withstand any adding to or taking away from the simple message of the Gospel of Christ.
>
> ...peace without truth is a false peace; it is the very peace of the devil. Unity without the Gospel is a worthless unity; it is the very unity of Hell.

Unity which is obtained by the sacrifice of truth is worth nothing. It is not the unity which pleases God....

Controversy in religion is a hateful thing.... But there is one thing which is even worse than controversy, and that is false doctrine tolerated, allowed, and permitted without protest or molestation.... There are times when controversy is not only a duty but a benefit. Give me the mighty thunderstorm rather than the pestilential malaria. The one walks in darkness and poisons us in silence, and we are never safe. The other frightens and alarms for a little season. But it is soon over, and it clears the air. It is a plain Scriptural duty to "contend earnestly for the faith once delivered to the saints" (Jude 3).[94]

Protestantism's "Alone's" Versus Rome's "And's"

As I begin to bring this monograph to a close, I must say, sadly, that where the Holy Scripture and classical Protestantism have placed their *solus* ("alone") (see their *sola scriptura, sola gratia, solus Christus, sola fide, soli Deo gloria*), Roman Catholic theology has continued to place its *et* ("and") (recall here its doctrines of Scripture *and* Tradition as its authority).

Rome's "And" in the Accomplishment of the Atonement

Rome has placed its "and" in its teaching on salvation when it insists that both God *and* man play a determining role in the *accomplishment* of salvation. But the Bible and classical Protestantism teach that Christ's saving work at Calvary was a "once for all" atoning work which he alone accomplished. Christ's cross-work satisfied divine justice once and for all

---

[94] J. C. Ryle, *Warnings to the Churches*, 105, 106, 110, emphasis in the original.

with respect to the sin of all those for whom he died, as witnessed by Holy Scripture and by the fact that God raised him from the dead, and it does not require any repetition:

Romans 6:10: "The death he died, he died to sin *once for all* [ἐφάπαξ, *ephapax*]."

Hebrews 7:27: "Unlike the other high priests, he does not need to offer sacrifices day after day.... He sacrificed for their sins *once for all* [ἐφάπαξ, *ephapax*] when he offered himself."

Hebrews 9:12: "He did not enter by means of the blood of goats and calves; but he entered the Most Holy Place once for all [ἐφάπαξ, *ephapax*] by his own blood, having obtained eternal redemption."

Hebrews 9:25-26, 28: "Nor did he enter heaven *to offer himself again and again*...now he has appeared *once for all* (ἅπαξ, *hapax*] at the end of the ages to do away with sin by the sacrifice of himself...so Christ was sacrificed *once for all* [ἅπαξ, *hapax*] to take away the sins of many people."

Hebrews 10:10-14: "...we have been made holy through the sacrifice of the body of Jesus Christ *once for all* [ἐφάπαξ, *ephapax*]... But when this priest had offered for all time *one sacrifice* for sins, he sat down at the right hand of God. Since that time he waits for his enemies to be made his footstool, because by *one sacrifice* he has made perfect forever those who are being made holy."

1 Peter 3:18: "For Christ died for sins *once for all* [ἅπαξ, *hapax*], the righteous for the unrighteous, to bring you to God."

And the author of Hebrews informs us that once we have received the forgiveness of sins by Christ's "once for all time sacrifice," "there is no longer any sacrifice for sins" (Heb 10:18).

Now the Roman Catholic priest can only be a priest either in the order of Aaron or in the order of Melchizedek since the Scriptures recognize no other priestly orders. Which one? Gratian's *Decretum* I. xxi and Peter Lombard's *Sentences* IV. xxiv. 8-9 declare that the Roman priest serves as a priest in the Aaronic order, as does the 1994 *Catechism of the Catholic Church*:

> The liturgy of the Church...sees in the priesthood of Aaron and the service of the Levites...a prefiguring of the ordained ministry of the New Covenant. ...At the ordination of priests, the Church prays: "Lord...You shared among the sons of Aaron the fullness of their father's power." (paragraphs 1541-42)

But then the Roman priest should understand that that priestly order has been superseded by the priestly order of Melchizedek and rendered obsolete (Heb 8:13) by the priestly order of Melchizedek which is founded upon a "better covenant" (Heb 7:22) and "better promises" (Heb 8:6), which introduces a "better hope" (Heb 7:19), and which serves with "better sacrifices" (Heb 9:23) "the greater and more perfect tabernacle that is not man-made" (Heb 9:11). About the Aaronic priestly system the author of Hebrews distinctly states:

Hebrews 7:11: "If perfection could have been attained through the Levitical priesthood..., why was there still need for another priest to come—one in the order of Melchizedek, not in the order of Aaron?"

Hebrews 8:6-7: "...the ministry Jesus has received is as superior to [the Aaronic ministry] as the covenant of which he is mediator is superior to the old one.... For if there had been nothing wrong with that first covenant, no place would have been sought for another."

Hebrews 9:9, 13-14: "...the gifts and sacrifices being offered [in the Aaronic order] were not able to clear the conscience of the worshiper...[their offerings made the worshiper only] outwardly clean. How much more, then, will the blood of Christ...cleanse our consciences from acts that lead to death, so that we may serve the living God."

Hebrews 10:1, 12, 14: "[The Aaronic sacrifices which can never take away sin, Heb 10:11] can never...make perfect those who draw near to worship.... But when [Christ] had offered for all time one sacrifice for sins, he sat down at the right hand of God...because by one sacrifice he has made perfect forever those who are being made holy."

In light of these biblical affirmations the Roman priest must face this question, and I am not trying to be cute when I pose it; I am very serious when I ask it: Is the Aaronic "sacrifice" that he makes in the Mass imperfect or perfect? If it is imperfect, then he must be able to explain why he is offering it, since it is incapable of clearing the conscience of the worshiper, can never take away sin, and can never perfect those who attempt to come to God by it? If it is perfect, then he must be able to explain how it is that he, an Aaronic priest, has a perfect sacrifice to offer when Aaron himself, the head of his order, never had such a sacrifice? Moreover, if it is perfect, then he must be able to explain why he needs to keep repeating it? For Christ sat down; his work was done! Why do the Roman priests still stand and offer him?

Should Rome respond to these questions by saying that its priests are also serving in the order of Melchizedek, then it must be said that the Roman priest serves in an earthly order created out of whole cloth that has no scriptural warrant whatsoever. Jesus Christ, being "holy, blameless, pure, set apart from sinners, exalted above the heavens" (Heb 7:26), is the *only* high priest in the order of Melchizedek, who as such is a priest *forever* (Heb 5:6; 6:20; 7:3, 17, 21), who possesses an "*indestructible* life" (Heb 7:16) and a "*permanent* priesthood" (Heb 7:24), who is "able to save *completely* those who come to God through him, because he *always* lives to intercede for them" (Heb 7:25), and who, unlike the high priests of the Aaronic order, "does not need to offer sacrifices day after day, first for his own sins, and then for the sins of the people" since "he sacrificed for their sins *once for all* when he offered himself" (Heb 7:27-28), that is, when "he entered the Most Holy Place *once for all* by his own blood, *having obtained eternal redemption*" (Heb 9:12). In other words, there is no further need for an earthly priesthood to continue to offer a carnal sacrifice to God, either animal or human. And nowhere does Scripture teach that he appointed within the Church a special order of priests to offer him again and again to the Father in and by the Mass. What Christ the heavenly high priest has done is to make his people—*all* of them—"priests to serve his God and Father" (Rev 1:6; 5:10; 20:6), indeed, he has made them a "*holy* priesthood, offering spiritual sacrifices acceptable to God through Jesus Christ" (1 Pet 2:5) and a "*royal* priesthood" that they "may declare the praises of him who called [them] out of darkness into his wonderful light" (1 Pet 2:9). Such people need no other priest before God than the one high priest Jesus Christ who is the propitiation for their sins and their Advocate before the Father at his right hand (1 John 2:1-2). Finally, if ministers of Jesus Christ have a "priestly duty" in this present age—and they surely do!—it is the "priestly duty" about which Paul writes in Romans 15:16, namely, the "duty of proclaiming the gospel of God, so that the Gentiles might become an offering acceptable to God, sanctified by the Holy Spirit" (see Isaiah 66:20), which is precisely the one duty which is *not* listed under the tasks of the priest in the *Catechism of the Catholic Church* (790). Charles Hodge correctly observes on Romans 15:16:

> In this beautiful passage we see the nature of the only priesthood which belongs to the Christian ministry. It is not their office to make atonement for sin, or to offer a propitiatory sacrifice to God, but by the preaching of the gospel to bring men, by the influence of the Holy Spirit, to offer themselves as a living sacrifice, holy and acceptable to God. It is well worthy of remark, that amidst the numerous designations of the ministers of the gospel in the New Testament, intended to set forth the nature of their office, they are never officially called priests. *This is the only passage in which the term is even figuratively applied to them*, and that under circumstances which render its misapprehension impossible. They are not mediators between God and man; they do not offer propitiatory sacrifices. Their only priesthood, as Theophylact says, is the preaching of the gospel,...and their offerings are redeemed and sanctified men, saved by their instrumentality. (Emphasis supplied)[95]

Is it any wonder that John Calvin declared that Rome is "attempting something ingenious: to shape one religion out of Christianity and Judaism and paganism [he refers here to

---

[95] Charles Hodge, *Commentary on the Epistle to the Romans* (Reprint of revised 1886 edition; Grand Rapids: Eerdmans, 1955), 439.

the "fiction" of transubstantiation[96] and the concomitant adoration of created things] by sewing patches together" (*Institutes*, 4.19.31), and that the unscriptural Roman priesthood as it goes about its offerings of an "unbloody sacrifice" in the myriad Masses it offers daily, blasphemes Christ, supp-

---

[96] Rome would want the world to believe that its doctrine of transubstantiation, which teaches that the Roman priest is empowered to transform the ordinary bread and wine at the Lord's Supper into the actual physical body and blood of Jesus Christ, goes back to Christ himself. Actually, the New Testament knows and the ancient church knew nothing about such a doctrine. It is a late medieval philosophical effort to explain a real presence of Christ in the Supper, physically perceived, which involves the changing of the *substance* of bread into the substance of Jesus' human flesh without changing the *accidents* of the bread (that is, the bread still looks, feels, tastes, and smells like bread)—a real philosophical conundrum. It first received canonical status at the Fourth Lateran Council in A.D. 1215 in order to counter the anti-clerical, anti-sacramental teachings of the Albigensians that were perceived as imperiling the medieval church, especially in France. It took two generations for the theological formulation of the doctrine to be worked out, with its full formulation finally being stated by Thomas Aquinas in his two *Summae*, and its liturgical expression established in the feast of Corpus Christi, for which Aquinas also wrote the service and the hymns.

Very quickly the Mass and its attendant "priestly miracle" became the linchpin of the whole medieval ecclesiastical system in the West. It had to stand unchallenged if the delicately poised system of Church and State was to survive, for to attack it in any way was to attack the entire ecclesiastical system resting upon it, which in turn made the State itself unstable and hence vulnerable to internal disintegration and/or external attack. Hence both Church and State in medieval times equally fought fiercely against any questioning of its validity or of any of its attendant features such as Rome's entire seven-fold sacramental system, indulgences, the treasury of merit, the invocation of saints, and purgatory.

The Reformers criticized this doctrine because of (1) the absence of any scriptural support for it; (2) the unwarranted authority that such a view places in the hands of men; (3) its lack of stress upon the role of faith in the reception of the ordinance's spiritual benefit, for conceived as working *ex opere operato* its benefits are ingested by the mouth and

resses the eternal power of his cross work to save sinners once and for all, wipes out the true and unique death of Christ, robs men of the benefit of his death, and nullifies the true significance of the Lord's Supper (*Institutes*, 4.18.2-7).

But in spite of these clear biblical affirmations Rome teaches that the Roman Catholic priest must continually "sacrifice" Christ for sins after baptism in and by the "unbloody sacrifice" of the Mass.[97] Moreover, Rome asks its communicants to commit idolatry when it instructs them that they should regard the bread and the wine after their consecration in the Mass as having become God the Son himself and to bow down and worship that which hands have made.[98] Regarding all such teaching the Scriptures are silent; the Lord's Supper is a sacramental *remembrance*, not a sacerdotal *reenactment!*

---

not by the heart governed by faith; (4) the Mass's implicit attack upon Christ's finished work at Calvary in its represented character as an offering of an "unbloody propitiatory sacrifice" to God; and (5) its "magical" character, since unlike the visible miracles of Christ and of the New Testament in general which could be seen by both believer and unbeliever alike, this "miracle" is not visible to anyone.

[97] In the second chapter of its Twenty-Second Session (September, 1562) the Council of Trent declares: "... inasmuch as in this divine sacrifice which is celebrated in the mass is contained and immolated [offered in sacrifice] in an unbloody manner the same Christ who once offered himself in a bloody manner on the altar of the cross, the holy council teaches that this is truly propitiatory.... For, appeased by this sacrifice, the Lord grants the grace and gift of penitence and pardons even the gravest crimes and sins. For the victim is one and the same, the same now offering by the ministry of priests who then offered himself on the cross.... The fruits of that bloody sacrifice...are received most abundantly through this unbloody one [and] it is rightly offered not only for the sins, punishments, satisfactions and other necessities of the faithful who are living, but also for those departed in Christ but not yet fully purified."

[98] In the fourth and fifth chapters of its Thirteenth Session (October, 1551) the Council of Trent declared that "by the consecration of the

Rome's "And" in the Application of the Atonement

Rome has done the same again when it places its "and" in the sphere of the *application* of salvation. The Bible teaches that Christ, by his Word and Spirit, applies the benefits of his redemption to his own, but Rome adds the "meritorious" work of Mary, not to mention the supererogatory work of its other saints, to this applicational work of the Godhead. In his papal encyclical *Redemptoris Mater* issued on March 25, 1987 Pope John Paul II teaches that Mary, having been assumed bodily into heaven and being absolutely pure and sinless (1) cooperates in her Son's work of redemption, (2) unceasingly intercedes for believers and for the world,[99] (3) protects God's people and the nations, and (4) reigns as Queen of the Universe. He writes:

---

bread and wine a change is brought about of the whole substance of the bread into the substance of the body of Christ our Lord, and of the whole substance of the wine into the substance of his blood," and that therefore "the faithful of Christ may...give to this most holy sacrament in veneration the worship of *latria*, which is due to the true God...For we believe that in it the same God is present of whom the eternal Father...says: *And let all the angels of God adore him*."

The *Westminster Confession of Faith*, XXIX/vi, declares: "That doctrine which maintains a change of the substance of bread and wine into the substance of Christ's body and blood (commonly called transubstantiation), by consecration of a priest, or by any other way, is repugnant not only to Scripture alone, but even to common sense and reason; overthroweth the nature of the sacrament; and hath been, and is, the cause of manifold superstitions, yea, of gross idolatries." This language may be considered by some as intemperate, but the doctrine it enunciates, it should be recognized, is Protestantism in its purest confessional expression. But how many professing Protestants are publicly saying this today? Very few, I fear.

[99] Do Roman Catholics not understand that to believe that Mary can hear the prayers of the millions of Catholic faithful who are praying to her at any one time in the myriad languages of the world, that she can

Mary's motherhood continues unceasingly in the Church as the mediation which intercedes, and the Church expresses her faith in this truth by invoking Mary "under the titles of Advocate, Auxiliatrix, Adjutrix, and Mediator." (39)

We believe that the Most Holy Mother of God, the new Eve, the Mother of the Church, carries on in heaven her maternal role with regard to the members of Christ, cooperating in the birth and development of divine life in the souls of the redeemed. (47)

She is also the one who, precisely as the "handmaid of the Lord," cooperates unceasingly with the work of salvation accomplished by Christ, her Son. (49)

Mary, though conceived and born without the taint of sin, participated in a marvelous way in the sufferings of her divine Son, in order to be Coredemptrix of humanity.

In this encyclical, by giving to Mary the titles he does, from Mediatrix to Morning Star, from Most Holy Mother of God[100] to Mother of the Church, from Advocate to Adjutrix, from Protector to Perfect Model, Pope John Paul II has taken the attributes and accomplishments rightly attributable only to the Father, to Christ, and to the Holy Spirit and has applied them to the sinful creature.

---

keep each prayer infallibly related to its petitioner, and that she can present these myriad petitions as they are prayed to her Son is to ascribe the divine attributes of omniscience to her? Do they not understand that they have deified her?

[100] I do not take exception to Mary being viewed as 'Godbearer' (*theotokos*). But I do take exception to the ascription to her of the divine attribute, 'Most Holy', and what it is intended to teach. Mary was not sinless, as Rome contends.

Nevertheless, he believes that this emphasis on Marian devotion and on "Mary's role in the work of salvation" will help the divided churches on their path toward unity:

> By a more profound study of both Mary and the Church, clarifying each by the light of the other, Christians who are eager to do what Jesus tells them—as their Mother recommends (cf. Jn. 2:5)—will be able to go forward on "this pilgrimage of faith." Mary, who is still the model of this pilgrimage, is to lead them to the unity which is willed by their one Lord and so much desired by those who are attentively listening to what "the Spirit is saying to the Churches" today (Rev. 2:7, 11, 17). (30)

Moreover, in the conclusion of his encyclical letter *Veritatis Splendor* (*The Splendor of Truth*) Pope John Paul II calls upon all the bishops of the Catholic Church to entrust themselves, not to Jesus Christ, but to Mary, "the Mother who obtains for us divine mercy" (para. 118, 120)!

The reality, however, is that there is no biblical warrant for such Marian devotion anywhere in Scripture. Nowhere does the Bible exalt Mary in the manner that Rome does. In fact, Mary needed a Saviour (Luke 1:47), as does all mankind. And the Gospel record suggests that she erred at times when she attempted to inject herself into her Son's ministry, for which Jesus always firmly reproved her (Luke 2:48-50; John 2:3-4; Matt 12:49-50; Mark 3:34-35). According to the Matthean and Markan passages just cited, our Lord, upon hearing that his mother and brothers were calling for him, pointed to his *disciples* and declared: "Here are my mother and my brothers. For *whoever* does the will of my Father in heaven is my brother and sister and mother." In Luke 8:21 he declared: "My mother and brothers are those who hear God's word and put it into practice." When a woman on another occasion said to him, "Blessed is the womb that bore you and the breasts that nursed you," he expressed the same sentiment: "On the contrary [Μενοῦν, *Menoun*], blessed are those who hear the word of God and obey it" (Luke 11:27-28). By these declarations Jesus implies that Mary's physical relationship to him as his biological mother, while not unimportant to him, was not all-important either. His disciples' doing the will of God, that is, hearing and obeying God's word, was what ultimately mattered to him, for such submission to God places one in Christ's *spiritual* family— a family that transcends any and every earthly familial relationship. His precious disciples Christ loved, cherished and honored as his "family" above even his biological family, including (at that time) Mary his mother. Which is just to say that his disciples comprise the only "family" within mankind that Jesus recognizes.

Moreover, Rome's idolatrous view of Mary is anything but a unifying feature in its theology. To the contrary, its unbiblical exaltation of Mary continues to be one of the major blocks to reunification of the church as it diminishes the uniqueness of Christ's saving work, weakens the sense of immediate access to Christ that is every Christian's birthright, and undermines the Pauline *solus Christus* and *sola fide* of justification. By its exaltation of Mary the Roman Catholic Church makes itself the largest cult in Christendom —the Marian cult.

Rome's "And" in Its Ecclesiology

Rome has done the same again when it teaches that the proper object of saving faith is Christ *and* the Roman church (which it would appear for most Catholics becomes faith in the Roman church and its sacraments). William F. Lynch, S.J., who describes the uniqueness of Roman Catholicism precisely in terms of its perception of the Roman church as the on-going incarnation of Christ, writes that "the Church

claims resolutely, scandalously, to be Christ Himself."[101]
Joseph Ratzinger speaks of the Roman church as "a single
subject with Christ."[102] "For the Catholic," Richard John
Neuhaus writes, "faith in Christ and faith in the Church are
one act of faith."[103] And the *Catechism of the Catholic
Church* asserts that "Christ and his Church...together make
up the "whole Christ" (*Christus totus*)."[104] Accordingly,
Friedrich G. E. Schleiermacher, professor of theology at
the University of Berlin who became the "father of liberal
theology", rightly observed many years ago: "For Protestants
the individual's relationship to the Church depends upon a
relationship to Jesus Christ, whereas in Catholicism the
reverse is true."[105] This is just to say that, according to Rome,
to have *implicit* faith that whatever the church teaches is
true and to submit to its teaching, even though Scripture is
silent on or opposed to such teaching and even though one
may not even know what the church teaches, is to have
explicit faith in Jesus Christ. Rome urges its faithful that
they need not fear committing themselves with implicit faith
to the church's teachings since the church's Magisterium
cannot err in matters necessary to salvation because, as the
continuing "whole Christ," it is being guided by the Holy
Spirit. Therefore, whatever dogma it proclaims, even if that

---

[101] William F. Lynch, "The Catholic Idea," in *The Idea of Catholicism*,
edited by Walter Burghardt and William F. Lynch (Expanded edition;
Cleveland: World, 1964), 59.

[102] Joseph Ratzinger, *Introduction to Christianity* (London: Burns &
Oates, 1969), 179.

[103] Richard John Neuhaus, "The Catholic Difference," in *Evangelicals
and Catholics Together: Toward a Common Mission*, edited by Charles
Colson and Richard John Neuhaus (Dallas: Word, 1995), 216.

[104] *Catechism of the Catholic Church* (Ligouri, Missouri: Ligouri,
1994), paragraph 795.

[105] Friedrich G. E. Schleiermacher, *The Christian Faith* (New York:
Harper Torchbooks, 1963), 103.

dogma cannot be found in the written Word of God, should still be accepted as a sure oracle of God.

Such teaching is erroneous in the extreme.[106] The Scriptures teach that the church in all its teaching must be subject to the written Word of God and that the Holy Spirit guides the church only by means of the written Word (John 15:12-15; 1 Cor. 2:13; 2 Tim. 3:15–4:2). This means that the church, if it makes its sole appeal to the Holy Spirit's guidance, cannot safely go its own way without the written Word. John Calvin, the sixteenth century Reformer, warned against this isolated appeal to the Holy Spirit as a colossal error that has done great harm to the church:

> ...it is easy to conclude how wrong our opponents act when they boast of the Holy Spirit solely to commend with his name strange doctrines foreign to God's Word—*while the Spirit wills to be conjoined with God's Word by an indissoluble bond*, and Christ professes this concerning him when he promises the Spirit to his church...[Christ] forbade anything to be added to his Word or taken away from it. It is this inviolable decree of God and of the Holy Spirit which our foes are trying to set aside when they pretend that the church is ruled by the Spirit apart from the Word.[107]

Rome grounds these teachings in its *theological* extrapolation from the *biblical* metaphor of the church as the "body of Christ" with Christ as its "head" and the Pope

---

[106] See John Calvin, *Institutes of the Christian Religion*, edited by John T. McNeill and translated by Ford Lewis Battles (Philadelphia: Westminster, 1960), "Prefatory Address to King Francis I of France," section 6, for his response to Rome's contention that the Roman pontiff and his bishops cannot err.

[107] John Calvin, *Institutes of the Christian Religion*, IV.8.13 (emphasis supplied).

as the vicar of Christ on earth so that the church is
objectively the mystical prolongation of the Incarnation and
as such has Christ's authority to issue its *Roma locuta, causa
finita est*—"Rome has spoken, the matter is settled"—in
doctrine. Hence for Rome the church is the proper object
of faith. The New Testament, however, employs more than
eighty metaphors for the church,[108] and the burden of proof
rests upon Rome to show that this image is the one image
among them that is to be construed not metaphorically but
literally. Moreover, in the New Testament the church always
preaches Christ and never self-reflectively itself (see, for
example, John 1:12; 3:16; Acts 5:42; 8:5; 9:20, 22; 18:5,
28; 26:22-23; 28:23, 31; Rom 10:13; 1 Cor 12:3; Col 1:28),
that is to say, the church's gospel is always theocentric and
christo-centric and never ecclesiocentric. In the New
Testament it is always Christ, never the church, who is the
single subject of salvific activities: it is he who loved (Eph
5:2), he who died for (Rom 5:6), he who gave himself for
(Tit 2:14), he who suffered for (1 Pet 2:21), he who
redeemed (Gal 3:13), he who quickens (John 5:21), he who
washes (Rev 1:5), he who grants repentance to (Acts 5:31),
he who gives eternal life to (John 10:28), he who gives peace
to (John 14:27), and he who nourishes and cherishes (Eph
5:29) the church. In the New Testament the church's call to
faith is always a summons to trust in Christ as Messiah and
Lord, as Redeemer and Savior (Acts 2:21; Rom 10:13).
Never does the New Testament church in its proclamation
self-reflectively represent itself in these roles as the object
of saving faith.[109] Indeed, faith itself in Christ is never

---

[108] See Paul Minear, *Images of the Church in the New Testament*
(Philadelphia: Westminster, 1960).

[109] The formula in the Apostles' Creed, "I believe in...[the] holy
catholic church" (πιστεύω εἰς...ἁγίαν καθολικὲν ἐκκλησίαν, *pisteuō
eis...hagian katholikēn ekklēsian*) and the Nicaeno-Constantin-

represented in the New Testament as the gift of the church but as the gift of God (Eph 2:8-9; Phil 1:29). Finally, in the New Testament "all authority" has been given, not to the church, but to Christ (Matt 28:19), and the church is to be subject to him as he has revealed himself through the writings of his apostles as authoritative teachers of doctrine. One must conclude with sadness that Rome's "high" ecclesiology, created in the interest of establishing its ecclesial stability, authority, and unshakeability, has correspondingly resulted in a "low" soteriology.

Rome's "And" in Its Eschatology

Rome teaches that the great mass of Christians, who are only imperfectly "justified" in this life, dying in communion with the church, go to purgatory after death where they "undergo purification [by suffering in the fires of purgatory], so as to achieve the holiness necessary to enter the joy of heaven" (*Catechism of the Catholic Church*, para 1030).[110] Rome's teaching on purgatory, based as we have already noted, on 2 Maccabees 12:46 and a very strained exegesis

opolitan formula of A. D. 381, "We believe in one holy catholic and apostolic church" (Πιστεύομεν εἰς μίαν ἁγίαν καθολικὴν καὶ ἀποστολικὴν ἐκκλησίαν, *Pisteuomen eis mian hagian katholikēn kai apostolikēn ekklēsian*) were intended by the early church fathers to affirm that Christians believe that there is such a church in the world, not that such a church is a saving object of trust alongside God the Father, God the Son, and God the Holy Spirit.

[110] On this subject the Creed of the Council of Trent (1564), a summary of Trent's doctrines and a creedal test to which, upon demand, every faithful Catholic must subscribe, states: "I, N., firmly hold that there is a purgatory, and that the souls detained therein are helped by the prayers of the faithful. I likewise hold that the saints reigning together with Christ should be honored and invoked, that they offer their prayers to God on our behalf, and that their relics should be venerated. I firmly

of 1 Corinthians 3:15, 1 Peter 1:7 and Jude 22-23, may be found in seed form in Tertullian where prayers for the dead are mentioned, in Origen who speaks of a purification by fire at the end of the world by which all men and angels are to be restored to favor with God, and in Augustine who did express doubt about some aspects of it. But it was specifically Gregory the Great who "reigned" on the papal throne from A.D. 590 to 604 who "brought the doctrine into shape and into such connection with the discipline of the church, as to render it the effective engine of government and income, which it has ever since remained."[111] It was finally formulated into and proclaimed an article of faith at the Councils of Florence (1439-1445) and Trent (1545-1563).

Rome also teaches, because it believes that "a perennial link of charity exists between the faithful who have already reached their heavenly home, those who are *expiating their sins* [*sic!*] in purgatory and those who are still pilgrims on earth" (emphasis supplied),[112] that Christians still living on earth can aid sufferers in purgatory to get to heaven by obtaining "indulgences" (temporal remissions of sin before God) on their behalf.[113] An elaborate doctrinal scheme underlies this teaching. Because the pope, it is said, holds

---

assert that images of Christ, of the Mother of God ever Virgin, and of the other saints should be owned and kept, and that due honor and veneration should be given to them. I affirm that the power of indulgences was left in the keeping of the Church of Christ, and that the use of indulgences is very beneficial to Christians." In light of what I will say later about relics, it is very important to note here that Trent endorsed the veneration of relics.

[111] Charles Hodge, *Systematic Theology* (Grand Rapids: Eerdmans, n. d.) III, 770.

[112] See *Catechism of the Catholic Church*, paragraphs 1471-9.

[113] The historical development of Rome's doctrine of indulgences is quite interesting. According to Loraine Boettner, *Roman Catholicism* (Philadelphia: Presbyterian and Reformed, 1962), 264-5:

"keys" given to him by Christ, these keys are obviously keys to something. To what? Rome teaches that the church is in possession of a "treasury of supererogatory merit" (*thesaurus supererogationis meritorum*) consisting of the infinite worth of Christ's redemptive work, "the prayers and good works [of supererogation] of the Blessed Virgin Mary"

The practice of granting indulgences was unknown to [the Greek and Latin Fathers]. It arose in the Middle Ages in connection with penances imposed by the Roman Church. At first they were applicable only to the living. Gelasius, bishop of Rome in 495, said: "They demand that we should also bestow forgiveness of sins upon the dead. Plainly this is impossible for us, for it is said, 'What things soever ye shall bind upon earth.' Those who are no longer upon the earth He has reserved for His own judgment." Now if this pope was infallible in his exegesis of Scripture, the current Roman practice is false. In the year 1096, at the Synod of Clermont, Urban II promised a plenary indulgence for all who would take part in the crusades. From that time on indulgences became a fixed and remunerative part of the religion of Rome. And in 1476 pope Sixtus IV declared that indulgences were available even for souls in purgatory.

In 1300 Boniface VIII issued a Jubilee Indulgence to all pilgrims who visited the tombs of the Apostles in Rome on 15 successive days (30 successive days were required of inhabitants of Rome). This Jubilee celebration turned out to be so spectacular and profitable that it could not be allowed to remain a memory. Originally limited to one-hundred-year intervals, the Jubilees became more and more frequent as papal financial difficulties deepened: Clement VI proclaimed the "treasury of merit" as expounded by Alexander of Hales to be church dogma in his bull *Unigenitus Dei Filius*, by which the church claimed authority to give one believer the excess merits of another, and he appointed a Jubilee celebration in 1350; Urban VI fixed its recurrence every 33 years in honor of Jesus' earthly career; and Paul II reduced the intervals to 25 years so that by 1900, under Leo XIII, the twentieth Jubilee was celebrated.

So the development was completed. By the beginning of the sixteenth century, when the magisterial Reformation occurred, indulgences had become a holy business (*sacrum negotium*) so extensive and complex as to demand the superintendence of the Banking House of Fugger.

which are "truly immense, unfathomable, and even pristine
in their value before God," as well as "the prayers and good
works [of supererogation] of all the saints" who by their
good works "attained their own salvation and at the same
time cooperated in saving their brothers in the unity of the
Mystical Body" (see Pope Paul VI's *Indulgentiarum
doctrina*, 5).[114] According to Romish dogma the pope has
the authority to declare the terms of indulgences, and in
exchange for the faithful Catholic's doing what the
indulgence requires of him the pope dispenses out of this
"treasury of the Church," through the administration of the
priests, the merits of Christ, of Mary and of the saints in
behalf of and for the benefit of loved ones suffering in
purgatory. This teaching points up as plainly as any teaching
could that Rome teaches that salvation is grounded in Christ's
merit plus Mary's and the saints' good works which also
have merit before God, plus their own expiatory suffering
in purgatory—all the expression of its philosophy of the
analogia entis in the sphere of soteriology.

---

[114] John Calvin dealt in his *Institutes*, 3.14.13-17, with the vanity of
believing that there can be "works of supererogation," by showing from
Scripture (1) that the one who speaks of "supererogatory" works
misunderstands the sharpness of God's demand and the gravity of sin,
(2) that even the perfect fulfillment of our obligation would bring us no
glory since we would have done "no more than what we ought to have
done" and are still only "unworthy servants [Δοῦλοι ἀχρεῖοι, *Douloi
achreioi*]" (Luke 17:10), (3) that, since God is entitled to all that we
are and have, there can be no supererogatory works, and (4) that when
we employ Aristotle's and Aquinas's "four kinds of causes," since the
efficient cause of our receiving eternal life is God the Father's freely
given love for us, the *material cause* Christ and his obedience through
which he acquired righteousness for us, the *instrumental cause* our
Spirit-given faith in Christ, and the *final cause* the demonstration of
God's justice and the praise of his glorious grace, it is plain that in no
respect can *our* works serve as the cause of our or anyone else's
righteousness or holiness.

With respect to the indulgence system itself, Philip Schaff, professor of church history at Union Seminary, New York, notes in his discussion of Rome's sale of indulgences in the Middle Ages that the expression *plena* or *plenissima remissio peccatorum* ("full remission of sins") occurs again and again in papal bulls granting such indulgences.[115] Such indulgences, confined mainly to the Germanic peoples of Europe, were granted for all sorts of purposes: for crusades against the Turks, for the building of churches, hospitals, and bridges, and for the repair of dikes. Among the more famous indulgences for the building of German churches were those for the rebuilding of the Cathedral of Constance, the building of the Dominican church in Augsburg and the St. Annaberg church, and the restoration of the Cathedral of Treves. And there were the indulgences granted for the building of St. Peter's Basilica in Rome. In this last case, according to Martin Luther, Tetzel the indulgence hawker, by the authority of Leo X, offered indulgences for the "complete absolution and remission of all sins," both for the living and the dead. Tetzel even declared that no sin— not even the sin of violating the Virgin Mary, if such a thing were possible, or a sin that one was *planning* to commit— was too great to be covered by the indulgence! Needless to say, such preaching led to great licence.

Always one-third to one-half of all indulgence money collected in these nations—from Switzerland and Austria to Norway and Sweden—would go to Rome. These vast sums of money were handled by the powerful Banking House of Fugger for a five-percent commission for changing the money, transmitting the money to Rome, and overseeing the money chests there. And this loathsome practice was carried out in spite of the fact that Peter, Rome's purported "first

---

[115] Philip Schaff, *History of the Christian Church* (Grand Rapids: Eerdmans, reprint of 1910 edition), VI, 756-7.

pope," had declared to his readers: "...it was not with perishable things such as silver and gold that you were redeemed from the empty way of life...but with the precious blood of Christ, a lamb without blemish or defect" (1 Pet 1:18-19). True, the Vatican's quite recent deliverance on indulgences, its *Enchiridion Indulgentiarum*, declares that the church will no longer sell indulgences as it did in the Middle Ages; *now Catholics are going to have to earn them by their good works!* This is less crass, perhaps, but hardly an improvement! It is still legalism.

Linked to the matter of indulgences is the related matter of the so-called Christian relics that also became a major source of income for those who collected them. And special indulgences were granted to those who collected these relics for the people's veneration. With the collection, for example, of the 8,133 relics at Halle billions of days of indulgence were associated. To be precise, the indulgences granted for the veneration of these relics were good for pardons totaling 39,245,120 years, and 220 days of suffering in purgatory! Even Wittenberg, Martin Luther's own city of professorial labor, had become a major relic center due to the zeal of Luther's protector, Duke Frederick, Elector of Saxony:

...Saxony had collected almost 18,000 relics, ranging from a twig from Moses' burning bush to a tear that Jesus shed when he wept over Jerusalem. Money from this traffic in relics provided the endowment for the University of Wittenberg. Pilgrims came from miles around, for by making the proper prayers and offerings, one could earn indulgences which would cancel out 1,902,202 years in purgatory.[116]

---

[116] Clyde L. Manschreck (ed.), *A History of Christianity: Readings in the History of the Church* (Grand Rapids: Baker, 1981), 2, 5.

In one of the best known of his treatises, "An Admonition, Showing the Advantages which Christendom Might Derive from an Inventory of Relics,"[117] John Calvin, endlessly and monotonously to accomplish his desired effect, enumerates, out of the four thousand dioceses, thirty thousand abbacies, forty thousand monasteries, and the multitude of parishes and chapels that existed then throughout Europe, the relics of which he was aware *in only six or so German cities, three or so cities in Spain, fifteen in Italy, and between thirty or forty in France* which were exposed for the veneration of the people. Since this treatise is not readily available to the Christian reading public, permit me to list some of the relics he mentions. With respect to Christ these relics included his teeth, his hair, his sandals, and his blood, not to mention the manger in which he was laid at birth, the swaddling clothes in which he was wrapped, the cradle in which his mother later laid him, the altar on which he was circumcised, and his foreskin—displayed at three different sites simultaneously (!); a picture of him when he was twelve years old, a pillar against which he leaned while disputing in the Temple, the water pots employed in his first miracle including some of the wine he created on that occasion, five pieces of the bread he created when he fed the five thousand, and the earth on which he stood when he raised Lazarus from the dead; the branch he purportedly carried when he rode into Jerusalem, the tail of the ass on which he rode, the table of the last Passover, some of the bread he broke on that occasion, the knife which was used to cut up the Paschal Lamb, two cups, one in a church near Lyons and one in an

---

[117] John Calvin, "An Admonition, Showing the Advantages which Christendom Might Derive from an Inventory of Relics," in *Selected Works of John Calvin: Tracts and Letters*, translated by Henry Beveridge and edited by Henry Beveridge and Jules Bonnet (Reprint; Grand Rapids: Baker, 1983), 287-341.

Augustinian monastery, both purported to have contained the sacrament of his blood, three dishes—at Rome, at Genoa, and at Arles—all three purported to have been the dish in which the Paschal Lamb was placed, the linen towel—one at Rome and another at Acqs, the latter with the mark of Judas' foot on it—with which he wiped the apostles' feet; the money which Judas received to betray Jesus and the steps of Pilate's judgment-seat (the steps Luther climbed); his cross the fragments of which if gathered together, Calvin estimated, would require more than three hundred men to carry; the tablet which Pilate ordered affixed over the cross—but displayed both at Rome and at Tholouse simultaneously; fourteen nails purported to be the nails driven into his hands and feet, the soldier's spear—but displayed at Rome, also at Paris, yet again at Saintonge, and still a fourth at Selve; the crown of thorns, a third part of which is at Paris, three thorns of which are at Rome, one at Vincennes, five at Bourges, three at Besançon, and three at Köningsberg, an unknown number in Spain, and twelve in almost as many cities in France; the robe in which Pilate clothed Christ located in at least four different sites; the reed placed in his hand as a mock scepter, the dice which were used to gamble for his robe but in appearance resembling more what we know today than what was known in Roman times, and the sponge containing vinegar mixed with gall which was offered to him at the cross; the napkin wrapped around his head in burial—but on display in eight different cities simultaneously, and a piece of the broiled fish Peter offered him after his resurrection, not to mention the numerous claims of possessing his footprints as well as crucifixes that grew beards, that spoke, and that shed tears.

With regard to Mary, two churches claimed to possess the body of her mother, while three churches claimed to possess one of her mother's hands. The churches displayed

Mary's hair, her combs, pieces of her wardrobe, four pictures of her purported to have been painted by Luke, a very valuable wedding ring purported to have been Mary's, and even vials of her milk, with so many towns, so many monasteries, so many nunneries laying claim here that, as Calvin writes, "had she continued to nurse during her whole lifetime, she scarcely could have furnished the quantity which is exhibited."

Six different churches claimed to possess the finger John the Baptist used when he pointed his disciples to Christ, while others claimed to possess his sandals, his girdle, the altar on which he purportedly prayed in the desert, and the sword that was used to cut off his head.

With regard to the apostles, the church at Lyons claimed to possess the twelve combs of the twelve apostles. Half of Peter's and Paul's bodies was said to be at St. Peter's, half at St. Paul's in Rome, while the heads of both were purportedly located in yet a third church. This did not stop other cities from claiming to have Peter's cheekbone, many bones belonging to both, and one claimed to have Paul's shoulder. Rome claimed to have the sword Peter used to cut off Malchus' ear, the "throne" on which he sat, the robe in which he was attired when he officiated at and the altar at which he said mass, the chain with which he was bound, and the pillar on which he was beheaded. Regarding the rest of the apostles, the church of Tholouse claimed to have six of their bodies, namely, those of James the Greater, James the Less, Andrew, Philip, Simeon, and Jude. But Andrew had another body at Melfi, Philip and James the Less had each another body at Rome, and Simeon and Jude had second bodies at St. Peter's. Bartholomew's body was exposed both at Naples and at Rome simultaneously. Three different churches claimed to have the body of Matthias, with a fourth claiming to possess his head and an arm. Most were purported to have body parts on display throughout the realms.[118]

The church even boasted of possessing relics of an angel—the dagger and shield of the angel Michael!

I will not weary the reader any longer by detailing an account of the thousands of other relics to which Rome laid claim—the Ark of the Covenant and Aaron's rod, the bones of Abraham, Isaac, and Jacob, the bodies of the Magi and of the Bethlehem "Innocents," the body of Stephen and those of other lesser known martyrs—only some of which Calvin methodically itemized in turn. It only remains for me to remind him, first, that Rome instructed the common people in Calvin's time that they should make their pilgrimages to these relic sites and revere these relics and employ them in their approach to and worship of God, and, second, that nothing has really changed since Calvin's day. For example, one is still shown today in the Church of St. Peter in Chains in Rome the chain that allegedly bound Peter; one is still shown in the Church of St. John Lateran in Rome the *Scala Sancta* that Christ allegedly climbed in his trial before Pilate (this church also claims to possess the heads of Peter and Paul); one is still shown and allowed to kiss in the Santa Chiara Cathedral in Naples the alleged vial of the martyred San Gennaro's powdered blood that supposedly "liquifies" every first Saturday in May and on September 19, the saint's feast day; one may still visit the "weeping" Madonnas in Civitavecchia, Italy, in Benin, France, in Rincon, Puerto Rico, in Wicklow, Ireland, and in scores and scores of other places, and seek miraculous healings from these pilgrimages. Little wonder that the unthinking masses adore

---

[118] It did not seem to trouble the fathers of Trent that the same object was venerated in different places. Jean Ferrand, the seventeenth-century Jesuit, even contended that such objects as the wood of the cross and the crown of thorns were so necessary for devotion to God that he arranged their miraculous replication.

them all as miracle workers and mediators between God and man, thereby diminishing Christ's sole mediatorship between God and man!

Protestants quite rightly reject entirely Rome's doctrines of purgatory, indulgences, and relics as being unscriptural and dishonoring to God. To suggest that a finite sinful creature could by his suffering for a finite number of years expiate the infinite disvalue of his sin against the one living, true, and holy God or could purchase indulgences for his own or another's sins is a pernicious error of massive proportions. Not only is it "another one of those foreign growths that has fastened itself like a malignant tumor upon the theology of the Roman Catholic Church,"[119] but also it is a doctrinal promulgation devised in the interest of sustaining the Roman Catholic priestcraft and the entire indulgence system of that church which is one of its chief sources of income.[120]

The Conflict Must Continue for the True Gospel's Sake!

All of these "and's" are outworkings of Rome's theologico/philosophical commitment to its Tradition, specifically to Thomas Aquinas's vision of the "analogy of being" (*analogia entis*) between nature and grace, and between creation and

---

[119] R. Laird Harris, *Fundamental Protestant Doctrines* [booklet], V, 7.

[120] At first blush one might conclude that the Romish teaching on purgatory would be so shocking to the Catholic mind that a steady departure from the Catholic church for Protestantism on this account alone would continually occur as Rome makes known to its young its teaching on purgatory. But further reflection on the fact that Rome's doctrine of purgatory contributes in its own way to fallen man's pride as it informs him that after death he will contribute to the accomplishment of his own salvation by means of his *expiating* suffering for his sins explains why men accept Rome's teaching on this terrible doctrine: the doctrine conforms to the thinking of their Pelagian hearts.

God, the former of which Rome regards, over against Reformation theology, as being still fundamentally good in spite of the Genesis fall. For myself, standing with the Reformers who contended that the first principle of all true theology is the fact that "God is there and he has spoken with finality in Holy Scripture," while I often disagree with the Swiss theologian Karl Barth, I do agree with him completely when he wrote: "I regard the *analogia entis* as the invention of Antichrist, and think that because of it one can not become Catholic."[121] For it is indeed the invention of Antichrist when one adds anything to the great *sola's* of the Bible and the Reformation. The "and" in "grace and...," "Christ and...," or "faith and..." evokes the apostolic curse and leads to the soul's damnation (Gal 1:6-9; 5:2-6; Rom 11:6)!

I do not deny, of course, that Protestantism has its faults[122] and perhaps in some quarters even some idolatry. But from formal *systematic* idolatry, I would contend, Protestantism as a doctrinal system is virtually free. This cannot be said for Roman Catholicism: "Romanism in perfection is a gigantic system of Church-worship, Sacrament-worship, Mary-worship, saint-worship, image-worship, relic-worship, and priest-worship,—...it is, in one word, a *huge organized idolatry.*"[123]

Accordingly, although there is little reason to believe that Pope John Paul II would heed my (or any other

---

[121] Karl Barth, "Foreword," *Church Dogmatics*, translated by G. T. Thomson (Edinburgh: T. & T. Clark, 1936), I/1, x.

[122] Roman apologists have incorrectly viewed modern theological liberalism and Barthianism as the natural fruits of the Protestant Reformation. Nothing could be further from the truth. Rome's own insistence on human free will and human freedom has contributed decisively to theological liberalism while Barthianism is a perversion of Reformation thought, indeed, a "new modernism."

[123] J. C. Ryle, *Warnings to the Churches*, 158, emphasis in the original.

Protestant's) urgings since he reaffirmed his confidence in Trent's deliverances on justification as recently as 1995, if I had a fifteen-minute private audience with him I would respectfully attempt to take him to Galatians 1:8-9 and urge him, first, to recognize that according to Paul the content of God's law-free gospel was already fixed by A. D. 49— indeed, it was already taught in the Old Testament (Gen 15:6; Ps. 32:1-2; see Rom 4:1-8)—and, second, for the sake of his own soul and the souls of the people of his communion, to repudiate the long stream of later additions which Romanism has added through the centuries to God's gospel of justification by faith alone, especially the Council of Trent's unevangelical, nomist, anti-Pauline teaching on justification, taking the church thereby away from the "sincere and pure devotion" (ἁπλότητος, *haplotētos*) which is in the Christ (2 Cor 11:3). And I would stress, because of these idolatrous additions, that he and all other Catholics are in peril of losing their souls.

I know that some readers will bristle at and be put off by my last remarks as being not only highly judgmental and irrational but also unbridled stridency and serious error since, they would remind me, the pope and the Roman Catholic faithful regularly confess their faith using the Apostles' Creed, the Nicene Creed, the Niceno-Constantin-opolitan Creed, the Definition of Chalcedon, and the Athanasian Creed. This observation is true enough, and I commend Rome for revering these early Creeds as valiant efforts to state and to protect the full unabridged deity of Jesus Christ and thus the triune character of the one living and true God. But what is overlooked is that these early creeds are not *evangelical* creeds, that is, creeds explicating soteric matters. As I just intimated, they were framed in the context of the Trinitarian and Christological debates in the fourth and fifth centuries and are sorely underdeveloped

respecting and virtually silent on soteriological matters. As
has been often pointed out, there is nothing in them that the
Judaizers whom Paul confronted in his letter to the Galatians
could not also have endorsed. Nevertheless, Paul condemned
the Judaizers in the strongest terms possible because they
were preaching "another gospel which is not another" when
they corrupted his doctrine of justification by faith alone.
Quite obviously, according to Paul there is no *saving* value
in holding to an "orthodox view" of the *person* of Christ if
one is at the same time also holding to an "unorthodox" view
of the *work* of Christ. Which is just to say that the question
of who Jesus is cannot be separated existentially from the
question of what he has done for us. And if Philip
Melanchthon is right when he said, "This is to know Christ:
to know his benefits," then one must even conclude that
Rome does not even know correctly who Christ really is!

In order that I might make myself crystal clear here—
and what I am now about to say may shock the reader but I
assure him that I do not say it for its shock value—I would
contend that one can believe from his heart that every
statement of the Apostles' Creed, the Nicene Creed, the
Niceno-Constantinopolitan Creed, the Definition of
Chalcedon, and the Athanasian Creed is true and *still be lost*,
if in order to be saved he is trusting to any degree in his own
character, and/or if he believes that he must contribute at
least some good works toward his salvation, and/or if he is
trusting in Christ plus anyone or anything else. Church history
is filled with too many examples of such "believers" for us
to ignore this fact, and they who so believe do so at the peril
of their own souls. Martin Luther as an Augustinian monk
confessed his faith many times during his monkish days using
the Apostles' Creed, but according to Scripture until he cast
himself in simple faith on Christ's saving work alone for his
justification before God he was lost. John Calvin in his early

years had the same experience. Until these men cast themselves in simple trust upon Christ alone they were unsaved. So one must clearly see that there is a danger in reciting even the revered, time-honored, truth-laden Apostles' Creed if one assumes that by simply believing its tenets one is thereby necessarily saved. For it is possible to believe the Apostles' Creed, and all the other Christological creeds as well, but also believe at the same time that if one would go to heaven when one dies one must still put some kind of an "and" or a "plus" of his own good works after Christ's perfect work of obedience. But they who would trust in the work of Christ *plus* their own "good works" that possess, as they are informed by Rome if they are Roman Catholics, "congruent merit" before God, *and/or* in the "pristine righteousness" and intercessory work of Mary and Rome's designated saints, *and/or* in their pilgrimages to Rome's designated holy sites, *and/or* in their earning of indulgences, according to Paul, as the Judaizers did before them, have made Christ's cross-work of no value to them (ὑμᾶς οὐδὲν ὠφελήσει, *humas ouden ōphelēsei*, Gal 5:2); they have been alienated from Christ (κατηργήθητε ἀπὸ Χριστοῦ, *katērgēthēte apo Christou*, 5:4a); they have fallen away from grace (τῆς χάριτος ἐξεπέσατε, *tēs charitos exepesate*, 5:4b); they have abolished the offense of the cross (κατήργηται τὸ σκάνδαλον τοῦ σταυροῦ, *katērgētai to skandalon tou staurou*, 5:11); they are trusting in a "different gospel which is no gospel at all" (1:6-7), and they are doing so at the peril of their souls, because they show thereby that they have never been truly regenerated by the Holy Spirit (or they would submit to the teaching of Holy Scripture alone in the matter of salvation[124]) but are still lost in their sin.[125]

---

[124] In light of John 4:41-42, 8:47, 1 Thessalonians 2:13, and 1 John 4:9-10, *Westminster Confession of Faith*, XIV/ii, reminds us that the

I am quite aware that if today a minister leads a quiet life, leaves the unconverted world and his misinformed Catholic friends alone, and preaches so as to offend no one, many will call him a "fine churchman." I am equally aware that when one expresses such opinions as these I have expressed in this monograph there will be many who will say: "He is no churchman; rather, he is a schismatic." I remain unmoved by such an accusation and believe that the Day of Judgment will show who were the true churchmen and who were not. For myself, I am convinced that they are the truest friends of Jesus Christ and his church who labor most for the preservation of the truth of the apostolic gospel even though they may be regarded in their own time as "firebrands" and "troublers in Israel." So, because Pelagianism, including in particular the modified form it takes today in Roman Catholicism, is always an attack on the *sola gratia, solus Christus*, and *sola fide* soteric principles, claiming as it does that man deserves at least some measure of credit for effecting his salvation, if not in its initiation, at least in his cooperation with initiating grace, and because Rome has given confessional Protestants no reason to anticipate any theological concessions on its part since its post-Vatican II teaching is a "seamless robe" which can brook no concessions without mortally damaging the whole, I would

---

Christian who has saving faith "believeth to be true whatsoever is revealed in the word, for the authority of God himself speaking therein."

[125] This is why the practice of some so-called "Protestant" evangelists who send their Roman Catholic converts back to the Roman Catholic Church is such a deplorable and scandalous compromise of the truth of the gospel. So-called "cooperative evangelism" that seeks Roman Catholic support for "evangelical" crusades does great harm in that it leaves every community in which it occurs in confusion as to what the true gospel is and where one should go to hear its proclamation. Such "cooperative evangelism" should be vigorously opposed by those who love the gospel that the apostles preached.

contend that the true church of Jesus Christ must ever be on guard to insure that the *sola gratia, solus Christus,* and *sola fide* soteric principles of Holy Scripture and of Paul specifically continue to be proclaimed as the sole ultimate way of salvation.

Furthermore, all the more is this vigilant proclamation necessary today since one has only to visit the great cathedrals of Europe, hear the Masses being said, and witness for himself the rows and rows of purchased burning candles "praying" for the souls in purgatory, or visit Fatima in Portugal, as I have, or Lourdes in southern France and observe the Roman Catholic superstitions evidenced there every day, and then try to find a Protestant church in those cities in order to hear the pure preaching of God's Word to realize that a doctrinal reformation is as sorely needed today within Christendom as it was in the sixteenth century in order to capture once again the glorious truth of the Pauline gospel of justification by grace alone through faith alone in Christ's preceptive and penal obedience.

Such a reformation can and will come only through *public* doctrinal conflict with Rome, openly pitting both in books, monographs, and pamphlets, and in sermons from the pulpit, first, the carefully exegeted, hermeneutically sound salvific teaching and world-and-life view of Holy Scripture against the superstitions and idolatries of Roman Catholic Tradition, and second, a sound knowledge of Rome's historical origins against its pretensions.[126] Protestants should not be afraid of such conflict, for the theological genius of the Reformation is really a summons to return to

---

[126] This second point reminds me of Robert L. Dabney's insightful comments in his address, "Uses and Results of Church History," in *Discussions: Evangelical and Theological* (Reprint; London: Banner of Truth, 1967), 2.13, made upon his induction into the professorship of ecclesiastical history and polity at Union Seminary, Hampden-Sidney, Virginia in 1854:

the simplicity of the apostolic gospel: from looking away from the institutional church to Christ, from looking away from Mary and Rome's many other intercessors to Christ the sole Advocate, from looking away from the "unbloody" Mass to the immeasurable worth of Christ's "once for all" bloody self-sacrifice, from looking away from the meritoriousness of our alleged good works to God's justification of the ungodly on the sole basis of Christ's doing and dying. In a day when the Roman Catholic Church is receiving "great press" in the Western media and growing throughout the world, it is high time for evangelical Protestant preachers and theologians civilly and warmly but also *publicly and firmly* to distinguish again for their people and the masses the Protestant faith from that of Roman Catholicism. For upon the doctrinal distinctives of the *"sola's"* of classic Protestantism hang the destinies of immortal souls.

...the best arguments against bad institutions are drawn from their history. The readiest way to explode unreasonable pretensions is to display their origin. Such an auditory as this need only be reminded that the battle against popery in the Reformation was fought on scriptural and historical grounds. Many of the most mortal stabs which Luther gave to mischievous popish institutions were by simply telling the ignorant world where and when they arose. And when the two hosts were regularly marshalled for controversy, there speedily came forth that great work, the parent of Protestant church history, the *Magdeburg Centuries* [thirteen volumes published from 1559 to 1574 under the editorship of Matthias Flacius—RLR]. This work, which was little more than a digest of ecclesiastical events, proved a grand historical argument against popery, and its effects were so deeply felt that Rome put forth her utmost strength in opposition to it, in the annals of Caesar Baronius. And now there is no better argument against popery than a simple history of its growth.

Appendix

Review of Robert A. Sungenis' *"Not by Faith Alone"*

Robert A. Sungenis has mounted a sustained argument for the Catholic teaching on justification in his *"Not By Faith Alone": The Biblical Evidence for the Catholic Doctrine of Justification* (Santa Barbara, CA: Queenship, 1997). He claims to have responded critically in his book to

> the writings of the major Reformation personalities such as Martin Luther, John Calvin, Francis Turretin, Philip Melanchthon, Martin Chemnitz, John Wycliffe, Huldreich Zwingli, Martin Bucer, Theodore Beza...Jonathan Edwards, and many other individuals, as well as groups such as...the Puritans. [The book] also analyzes documents such as the Formulas of Concord, the Augsburg Confession and its Apology, and many of the Reformed confessions and catechism. (xli)

His critiques, he then declares,

> are heavily concentrated on...representative spokesmen, especially those from the Reformed persuasion, including: Paul Althaus, John Armstrong..., Hermann [*sic*] Bavinck, Joel Beeke, Donald Bloesch, James M. Boice, James Buchanan..., Edmund Clowney, D. Clair Davis..., Sinclair Ferguson..., Ronald Fung, Richard Gaffin, Norman Geisler, John Gerstner, W. Robert Godfrey..., Charles Hodge..., Michael Horton, Philip E. Hughes, D. James Kennedy, George Eldon Ladd, R. C. H. Lenski, John MacArthur, J. Gresham Machen..., John Murray, J. I. Packer, John W. Robbins..., R. C. Sproul..., Robert Strimple..., Robert Zins, and many others. (xli)

These two lists include the names of some of the most learned thinkers in the history of Protestant thought, yet at the time of writing his seven-hundred-and-seventy-four-page book Sungenis' highest earned degree was a Masters degree from Westminster Theological Seminary! To say the least, his claim overreaches his book's actual accomplishments.

This present monograph is not the place to respond in detail to Sungenis' book, but I will say this much: I cannot remember ever reading a more transparently *eisegetical* treatment of any biblical doctrine in my professional life. While Sungenis reflects a broad general knowledge of contemporary theological currents, what surface scholarship his book exhibits serves only as a cover for his prejudice against the great exegetical insights and reasoning of the original Reformers and their more recent heirs.

The book gives the appearance of great learning, appealing constantly to the Greek text, but Sungenis often refuses to face the obvious meaning of the original text. Just two examples: Commenting on Jesus' parable of the Pharisee and the tax collector (Luke 18:9-14), he states that the tax collector's "going up to the temple to pray" was probably an "ongoing" daily activity even though the verb translated "going up" (ἀνέβησαν, *anebēsan*) is aoristic, that is, an action viewed as a single whole or as action occurring at a point. Nothing in the context suggests that the tax collector regularly went up to the temple to pray. Sungenis then goes on to say that what the tax collector did was to bring "his works before God with sincere faith and love" (197). And "under grace, his works are accepted...[but] if he sins again..., he will have to return to the temple and confess his sin, lest his justification be nullified...nothing in the passage proves a once-for-all imputed justification by *faith alone*" (198). This is, to say the least, shockingly poor exegesis; indeed, it is not *exegesis* at all, for *nothing* in the passage bears out his interpretation. It is the Pharisee who brought "his works before God" and from his perspective he doubtless did it "with sincere faith and love"; it is precisely the tax collector who did *not* bring his works before God (except for his sinful ones), but to the contrary he stood some distance away and, not willing even to lift his eyes toward heaven, he beat his breast and acknowledged himself to be "the sinner" and begged for God's mercy.

What *does* Jesus teach in this parable? Jesus elucidates his teaching on justification by declaring that the tax collector, who had simply prayed sincerely, "God, *have mercy* [ἱλάσθητι, *hilasthēti*] on me, the sinner," "went home *justified* [δεδικαιωμένος, *dedikaiōmenos*]." Jesus' first verb, ἱλάσθητι, *hilasthēti*, is the aorist passive imperative from ἱλάσκομαι, *hilaskomai*, "to propitiate," meaning here "be propitiated [now and forever]." Since its root is the same root which underlies ἱλασμός, *hilasmos*, "propitiation" (1 John 2:2; 4:10), and ἱλαστήριον, *hilastērion*, "propitiation" (Rom 3:25) and "mercy seat" (LXX, Ex 25:16; Lev 16:5; Heb 9:5), I would suggest that Jesus' tax collector is praying: "Look upon me mercifully, now and forever—the sinner that I am—as you do when you look at the sinner through the shed blood of the mercy seat." Jesus' second verb, δεδικαιωμένος, *dedikaiōmenos*, the perfect passive participle from δικαιόω, *dikaioō*, "to justify," means literally "*having been* justified." The force of the perfect tense in Greek is to represent an action as *complete whose finished result continues to exist.* Here Jesus teaches the *instantaneous* once-for-all-time justification of the penitent sinner through the instrumentality of the simple prayer of faith that looks for God's forgiveness on the ground of the shed blood of the sacrifice. And we can be sure, if this is what Jesus taught about justification, that he would not have led his inspired apostles to teach something else later. Surely this was Paul's doctrine of justification too!

At the outset of his study, it is true, Sungenis makes much of the two facts that Paul never employs the phrase "faith alone" and that the only place where the phrase "faith alone" (πίστεως μόνον, *pisteōs monon*) does occur it is preceded by the words "not by" (οὐκ ἐκ, *ouk ek*) (James 2:24)—hence the title of his book. But these facts had hardly escaped the attention of Martin Luther and John Calvin, both of whom had heard the same things said in their day and who had spoken directly to the objection. Luther observes:

> Note...whether Paul does not assert more vehemently that faith alone justifies than I do, although he does not use the word *alone* (*sola*), which I have used. For he who says: Works do not justify, but faith justifies, certainly affirms more strongly that faith justifies than does he who says: Faith alone justifies...Since the apostle does not ascribe anything to [works], he without doubt ascribes all to faith alone.[127]

Calvin, acknowledging that μόνος (*monos*) does not appear in Paul's exposition of justification by faith, urges that the thought of "faith alone" is nonetheless there:

> Now the reader sees how fairly the Sophists today cavil against our doctrine, when we say that man is justified by faith alone. They dare not deny that man is justified by faith because it recurs so often in Scripture. But since the word "alone" is nowhere expressed, they do not allow this addition to be made. Is it so? But what will they reply to these words of Paul where he contends that righteousness cannot be of faith unless it be free? How will a

---

[127] Martin Luther, *What Luther Says*, edited by Ewald M. Plass (St. Louis: Concordia, 1959), 2, 707-8.

free gift agree with works? ...Does not he who takes everything from works firmly enough ascribe everything to faith alone. What, I pray, do these expressions mean: "His righteousness has been manifested apart from the law"; and, "Man is freely justified"; and, "Apart from the works of the law"?[128]

Sungenis cites neither of them on this point and thus fails to answer them directly. In fact, he has not even answered Calvin's treatment of justification by faith alone that he gave almost four hundred and fifty years ago in his *Institutes*, 3.11-19. But quite clearly, since Paul never represents faith in Christ as a work but rather as a divine gift whereby the sinner looks away from himself and his work to Christ's doing and dying, and since Paul always sets faith in Christ— that is, the receiving and resting upon what God has done for us and freely offers to us in Christ—over against even our *good* works (Titus 3:5), then it must be by faith alone that sinners are justified.[129] And anyone who looks not only to the work of Christ but also to his own "good" works for his justification and/or counsels others that they must do the same becomes guilty of the same heresy that the Judaizers committed in the churches of Galatia and thus falls under the Pauline anathema of Galatians 1:8-9.

But since James' statement in James 2:24, as the title of Sungenis' book bears witness, is quite significant for him, I must say something about James' statement. What does he mean by his statement: "You see that a person is justified by what he does and not by faith alone" (2:24)? It has always

---

[128] John Calvin, *Institutes of the Christian Religion*, 3.11.19.

[129] See Paul's sustained emphasis on justification by faith in Christ as alone the justifying instrument in Gal 2:16; 3:1-14, 22-24; 5:2-11; 6:12-16; Rom 1:17; 3:20-22, 24, 28; 4:2-12; 5:1, 12-19; 8:1, 28-39; 9:30-32; 11:6; 2 Cor 5:21; Eph 2:8-9; Tit 3:5.

been urged by Roman Catholic apologists (see Council of Trent, Sixth Session, Chapters VII, X) that James 2:14-26 is a corrective to the Protestant (not the Pauline) "heresy" that justification is through faith alone completely apart from works, for James expressly declares: "You see that a man is justified by works, and *not* by faith alone [ἐξ ἔργων δικαιοῦται ἄνθρωπος καὶ οὐκ ἐκ πίστεως μόνον, *ex ergōn dikaioutai anthrōpos kai ouk ek pisteōs monon*]" (2:24). But an exacting exegetical analysis of James' teaching will disclose, as John Murray states, that "in James the accent [falls] upon the *probative* character of good works, whereas in the Pauline polemic the accent falls without question upon the judicially constitutive and declarative [character of justification]."[130] Paul and James clearly mean something different by their use of the words "justified," "faith," and "works," and they turn to different places in Genesis and thus to different events in Abraham's life to support their respective applications of Genesis 15:6. This much should be denied by no one.

Whereas Paul intends by "justified" the *actual* act on God's part whereby He pardons and imputes righteousness to the ungodly, James intends by "justified" the verdict which God *declares* when the *actually* (previously) justified man has *demonstrated* his actual righteous state by obedience and good works.[131]

Whereas Paul intends by "faith" trustful repose in the merits of Christ alone for pardon and righteousness, James is addressing those whose "faith" was tending toward, if it

---

[130] John Murray, "Appendix A: Justification," *The Epistle to the Romans* (Grand Rapids: Eerdmans, 1968), 1, 351.

[131] That a distinction must be drawn between God's *actual* act of justification whereby he pardons and constitutes the sinner righteous and his subsequent *declaring* acting of justification whereby he openly acquits the justified sinner before others is borne out by our Lord's

had not already become, a cold, orthodox intellectualism in which bare assent is given to such propositions as "God is one"—which even the demons confess with seemingly greater appreciation, for they tremble (2:19)—but which is devoid of any exhibition of love for the brethren.

Whereas Paul, when he repudiates "works," intends by "works" "the works of the law," that is, *any and every work of whatever kind* done for the sake of acquiring merit, James intends by "works" acts of kindness toward those in need performed as the fruit and evidence of a true and vital faith and the actual justified state (2:14-17).

Whereas Paul is concerned with the question, how may a man achieve right standing before God, and turns to Genesis 15:6 to find his answer, James is concerned with the question, how is a man to *demonstrate* that he has *true* faith and is therefore *actually* justified before God, and turns to Genesis 22:9-10, as the *probative* "fulfillment" of Genesis 15:6 (see Gen 22:12), to find his answer (2:21). Note his δεῖξόν [*deixon*, "show me"] and δείξω [*deixō*, "I will show you"] in 2:18; his βλέπεις [*blepeis*, "you see"] in 2:22; and his ὁρᾶτε [*horate*, "you see"] at the beginning of 2:24— the very verse under discussion: "*You see* that a man is justified by [his] works, and *not* by [his] faith alone".

---

actions in connection with the woman who washed his feet in Luke 7:36-50. He openly declares to Simon the Pharisee and to the woman herself that her many sins were forgiven (vss 47-48) "because she loved much [ὅτι ἠγάπησεν πολύ, *hoti ēgapēsen polu*]" (vs 47). But it is apparent that she had already been *actually* forgiven on some previous occasion because her acts of devotion toward him—the fruit and evidence of a lively faith—were due, he states, to her having already had "her debt canceled" (vss 41-43). The chain of events then is as follows: On some previous occasion Jesus had forgiven her (this was her *actual* justification, and Paul's concern). This provoked in her both love for him and acts of devotion toward him. This outward evidence of her justified state evoked from Christ his open declaration to Simon that she was forgiven (her *declared* justification, the interest of James).

Finally, whereas Paul believed with all his heart that men are justified by *faith alone in Christ*, he, as forthrightly as James does (2:17, 26), insists that faith, *if alone*, is not true but counterfeit faith: "For in Christ Jesus neither circumcision nor uncircumcision means anything. [What counts] is *faith working through love* [πίστις δι᾽ ἀγάπης ἐνεργουμένη, *pistis di᾽ agapēs energoumenē*]" (Gal 5:6), which expression is hardly different in meaning from James' expression: "*You see* that [his] faith was working with [Abraham's] works, and by works [his] faith was brought to its goal [βλέπεις ὅτι ἡ πίστις συνήργει τοῖς ἔργοις αὐτοῦ καὶ ἐκ τῶν ἔργων ἡ πίστις ἐτελειώθη, *blepeis hoti hē pistis sunērgei tois ergois autou kai ek tōn ergōn hē pistis eteleiōthē*]" (2:22). Paul can also speak of the Christian's "*work* of faith [τοῦ ἔργου τῆς πίστεως, *tou ergou tēs pisteōs*]," that is, construing the genitive as a subjective genitive, "the work produced by or originating from faith" (1 Thess 1:3). And in the very context where he asserts that we are saved by grace through faith and "*not by works* [οὐκ ἐξ ἔργων, *ouk ex ergōn*]" Paul can declare that we are "created in Christ Jesus *for good works* [ἐπὶ ἔργοις ἀγαθοῖς, *epi ergois agathois*] which God prepared beforehand that we *should walk in them*" (Eph 2:8-10). In sum, whereas for James "faith without works is dead," for Paul "faith working through love" is inevitable if the faith being considered is true faith, which amounts to exactly the same thing, only stated somewhat more positively. Clearly, there is no contradiction between them (see *Westminster Confession of Faith*, XVI: "Of Good Works"). Both Paul and James believed in justification by faith alone; both believed that faith without works, as probative evidence of that faith, is dead faith.

But for the sake of argument, let us imagine for a moment the impossible. Let us imagine that Sungenis demonstrated to the satisfaction of the *entire* Christian world that justification is, as Catholicism maintains, not by faith alone in Christ but by faith in Christ plus human efforts looked upon by God as possessing congruent merit (which is what most of professing Christendom believes already anyway). Such a demonstration would still not warrant anyone becoming a Roman Catholic. For far from the Roman Catholic Church being the *sole* depository of the "fullness of grace and truth" as it contends in the Vatican document entitled, "Declaration 'Dominus Iesus' On the Unicity and Salvific Universality of Jesus Christ and the Church," sections 16 and 17, dated August 6, 2000,[132] it is, within professing Christendom, the ecclesiastical epitome of serious doctrinal error. Its theology is systemically filled with all kinds of idolatries in connection with its doctrines of transubstantiation and the mediation of Mary and the saints, its images and relics, and its works salvation, and it makes idolaters out of virtually everyone who enters into its communion. And idolaters do not go to heaven.

But what makes Sungenis' entire effort such a tragic irony are two facts: first, that several of Roman Catholicism's most competent modern biblical scholars (for example, Brendan Byrne, a Jesuit and member of the Pontifical Biblical Commission, Joseph Fitzmyer, professor emeritus of biblical studies at the Catholic University of America, and Raymond E. Brown, late professor emeritus of biblical studies at Union Theological Seminary, New York) concede that the Pauline δικαιόω (*dikaioō*) has primarily and fundamentally a forensic meaning (to declare righteous);

---

[132] Hans Küng, dissident Swiss theologian who has been disciplined in the past by the Vatican for his rejection of papal infallibility, described this document as "a mixture of medieval backwardness and Vatican megalomania," and declared that it was hypocrisy on Rome's part to "continually talk about dialogue, while not talking about this colossal presence of absolutism."

and, second, that the very same document of the Second Vatican Council, the *Dogmatic Constitution on the Church* (1964), that asserts on the one hand Trent's medieval doctrine of justification, as Nick Needham has noted and has described as the "ultimate paradox," also makes the entire doctrine irrelevant on the other by teaching that all sincere people are saved, whatever their faith or lack of it (see paragraph 16)! Needham writes:

> An official footnote [to paragraph 16] elaborates: 'The Council is careful to add that men unacquainted with the biblical revelation, and even those who have not arrived at explicit faith in God, may by the grace of Christ attain salvation if they sincerely follow the lights God gives them.'
>
> With one blow, everything that modern Rome teaches about justification is short-circuited. Frankly, who cares what anyone thinks Scripture means by *dikaioo* when everyone can be saved by sincerity? Apparently, even the sincere atheist, who has not arrived at an explicit knowledge of God, can be saved as long as he lives a good life. By responding to the light of conscience, he is (without knowing it) responding in a salvific way to Christ.[133]

As a result of such blatant unbelief on Rome's part, within Roman Catholicism today may be found Tridentine conservatives, crypto-Lutherans, moderate liberals, and outright syncretists, with Rome's over-all drift being toward total religious pluralism. Why, therefore, some professing evangelical Protestants such as Sungenis have found Roman Catholicism attractive and have converted to present-day Rome is a complete mystery. For the Catholicism "to which most of them think they are converting—Thomistic,

---

[133] Dr. Nick Needham, "Have I Become Your Enemy By telling You The Truth?, *CRN JOURNAL*, Issue 6 (summer 1999), p.31.

Tridentine and devoutly Christian (at least in a historic creedal sense)—no longer exists. And even if such a Rome existed, it would still be the wrong choice, until or unless it reformed its official teaching about justification."[134]

It is regrettable that Surgenis'attack on biblical truth ever saw the light of day, but it is equally regrettable that his effort is hailed by Scott Hahn as providing "the solid scriptural grounds for the Catholic Church's teaching on Justification" (xiii) and by Thomas Howard as "a major document, noteworthy...for its punctilious scholarship" (xiv), for when I consider Sungenis' exegesis, even taking into account that his book received the *Nihil Obstat* and *Imprimatur* of two Catholic monsignors, my studied conviction is that whatever else these three men may be they are certainly *not* great biblical exegetes. So with Paul I would say to Sungenis, as well as to Hahn and Howard, all three of whom were Protestant Evangelicals but who have converted recently to Roman Catholicism:

> You foolish Galatians! Who has bewitched you? Before your very eyes Jesus Christ was clearly portrayed as crucified. I would like to learn just one thing from you: Did you receive the Spirit by observing the law, or by *believing what you heard?* Are you so foolish? After beginning with the Spirit, are you now trying to attain your goal by human effort?...Does God give you his Spirit and work miracles among you because you observe the law, or because you *believe what you heard*? (Gal. 3:1-5)

I would also ask these gentlemen to justify biblically their church's Old Testament priesthood and its on-going Mass work in light of the teaching of Hebrews 7–10 about Christ's definitive once-for-all cross work.

[134] Needham, *Ibid.*

SUBJECT INDEX

"Alexandrian canon," Gleason L. Archer, Jr. on 25.

Anathema, Pauline meaning of 20 fn 12.

"And's," Rome's: dire effects of 127; in Christ's accomplishment of the atonement 98-105; in Christ's application of the atonement 106-9; in its ecclesiology 109-13; in its eschatology 113-16.

Anselm, illustration of the elect remnant 76 fn 75.

Apocryphal books: attitude of Palestinian Jews toward 25; Rome's basis for prayers for the dead 27 fn 18; disclaimers of about themselves 24; inaccuracies of inconsistent with the nature of inspired Scripture 26-7; Merrill F. Unger on the phenomena of 18; Protestant view of 23-8; R. Laird Harris on 28; Roger Beckwith on 28; Rome's view of 21-3; teachings of at variance with inspired Scripture 27.

Apostasy, church's drift into soteriological 78-85.

Apostles' Creed 20, 86, 112, 125, 126, 127

Apostolic Fathers: Adolf von Harnack on 68; Benjamin B. Warfield on 69; C. N. Moody on 74; doctrinal trajectory of 67-78; James I. Packer on 74 fn 71; James Orr on 69; J. L. Neve on 72; J. N. D. Kelly on 72; Kenneth Escott Kirk on 68; Louis Berkhof on 71-2; Michael Green on 75; Richard Lovelace on 72; Thomas F. Torrance on 72-4.

Aquinas, Thomas: David S. Schaff on 83 fn 84; John Calvin on 83 fn 84; John H. Gerstner on 82 fn 83; Martin Luther on 83 fn 84.

Athanasian Creed 140, 141

Attributes of Scripture 28-9; Protestantism's view of 28-9; Rome's rejection of 28-9.

Augustinianism (see Pelagianism): teaching of 78.

Authority: Rome's twofold 21-31; problem with 30; transmissibility of Peter's 35.

PERSONS INDEX

SCRIPTURE INDEX

Acts, continued
15	34, 40, 42
15:1	11
15;5	11
18:5	112
18:28	112
26:22-23	112
28:23	112
28:30	36
28:31	112

Romans
1:11-13	41
1:17	82, 135
3:2	25
3:20	15
3:20-22	14, 135
3:24	135
3:25	133
3:25-26	16
3:26	15
3:28	15, 135
4:1-8	125
4:2-6	15
4:2-12	136
4:5	16, 88
4:6-7	18
4:13-14	16
4:23	88
5:1	18, 135
5:5	90
5:6	112
5:12-19	135
5:15	88
5:17	88
5:18	88
5:19	18, 88
6:10	99
8:1	135
8:28-39	135
9:12	15

9:30-32	16, 135
9:32	15
10:4	16
10:13	112
11:5-6	17
11:6	15, 124, 135
15:16	103
15:20	41

1 Corinthians
1:10-13	41
2:13	39, 111
3:3-9	41
3:11	49
3:15	114
9:5	37
10:4	49, 53
12:3	112
15:5	34

2 Corinthians
5:21	18, 135
10:16	41
11:3	125
13:10	39

Galatians
1:6	67
1:6-7	127
1:6-9	124
1:8-9	20, 125, 135
2:2	40
2:6	40
2:7-8	37
2:9	34, 40
2:11-14	39
2:12	11
2:14	39
2:16	15, 17, 135
3:1-14	135
3:1-5	141

3:2	15
3:5	15
3:10	15
3:10-11	17
3:13	112
3:22-24	135
4:16	141
5:2	127
5:2-6	124
5:2-11	135
5:4	127
5:6	138
5:11	127
6:12-16	135

Ephesians
2:8-9	17, 113, 135
2:8-10	138
2:9	15
2:20	53
5:2	112
5:29	112

Philippians
1:29	113
2:20-21	37
3:9	17

Colossians
1:28	112

1 Thessalonians
1:3	138
2:13	39, 127

2 Thessalonians
2:15	30, 39

1 Timothy
2:5	88